MURDER ON EASEY STREET

MURDER ON EASEY STREET

MELBOURNE'S MOST NOTORIOUS COLD CASE

HELEN THOMAS

NERO

Published by Nero,
an imprint of Schwartz Publishing Pty Ltd
Level 1, 221 Drummond Street
Carlton VIC 3053, Australia
enquiries@blackincbooks.com
www.blackincbooks.com

9781760640040 (paperback)
9781743820780 (ebook)

A catalogue record for this book is available from the National Library of Australia

Cover design by Nanette Backhouse, saso.creative
Inside front and back cover photos © Fairfax Syndication and Victoria Police
Text design and typesetting by Tristan Main

For Sue and Suzanne –
and justice, belated.

CONTENTS

PROLOGUE xi

CHAPTER 1 **THE MOVE** 1

CHAPTER 2 **THE MURDERS** 17

CHAPTER 3 **THE NEIGHBOURS** 23

CHAPTER 4 **THE DETECTIVES** 31

CHAPTER 5 **THE EXAMINERS** 41

CHAPTER 6 **THE FAMILIES** 49

CHAPTER 7 **THE 'VISITORS'** 57

CHAPTER 8 **THE NEIGHBOURS** 67

CHAPTER 9 **THE WITNESSES** 75

CHAPTER 10 **THE NEWSPAPERS** 93

CHAPTER 11 **THE SUSPECTS** 113

CHAPTER 12 **THE MEDIUM** 131

CHAPTER 13 **THE BOOK** 139

CHAPTER 14 **THE LETTERS** 147

CHAPTER 15 **THE HUNT** 159

CHAPTER 16 **THE SCIENCE** 167

CHAPTER 17 **THE REWARD** 179

CHAPTER 18 **THE THEORIES** 189

CHAPTER 19 **THE REASSESSMENTS** 197

CHAPTER 20 **THE HOUSE** 207

CHAPTER 21 **THE LEGACY** 221

CHAPTER 22 **THE HOPE** 233

AFTERWORD 239

NOTES 241

BIBLIOGRAPHY 251

ACKNOWLEDGEMENTS 257

‘We tell ourselves stories in order to live.’

—Joan Didion

PROLOGUE

It was a night like many others that summer in Melbourne, the kind of gentle January evening everyone enjoys. And Martin Bartlett was doing a favour for his sister. Always good at fixing things, he was hooking up the speaker leads to Susan's stereo, a task that seemed to elude the high-school teacher and her housemate, Suzanne Armstrong.

The two women, friends who grew up together in the Victorian country town of Benalla, had been sharing the small worker's cottage in Collingwood for just a couple of months, with Martin a regular visitor. He and his older sister saw each other – or at least spoke – once a week, and he was happy to perform brotherly tasks like this one. He was usually repaid with a home-cooked meal, and this night was no exception; plus, he just liked visiting Sue, as family and friends called her, and this evening had brought his girlfriend with him.

The house in Easey Street was neat and simple, with a patch of lawn in the backyard providing a comfortable backdrop for the blow-up pool the girls would fill with water on hot days for Suzanne's sixteen-month-old son, Gregory, to play in. Some of the young children in the street would jump into it too, running up the old 'dunny lane' along one side of the house and in through the open side gate to join him for a quick splash.

Having successfully fixed the stereo, and enjoyed their evening together, Martin Bartlett left his sister's house on 10 January 1977, and all was quiet, all was normal. Gregory was asleep in his cot in the small sewing room that doubled as his bedroom, and the two friends were getting ready to watch television. Just before Martin and his partner left, he and Sue made a loose plan to have dinner again soon, while Suzanne chatted to her younger sister on the phone.

Not a hint of anything out of the ordinary that Monday night, then.

Next door, Ilona Stevens and a friend from work at the *Truth* newspaper were playing pool in the back room of the cottage that was the mirror image of Sue and Suzanne's house. They were sharing a few after-dinner drinks and the easy comradery of colleagues who got on well, in and out of the office.

In the house on the other side of 147 Easey Street, the two properties separated by the short laneway, an elderly woman was getting ready for bed and tending to her ailing husband. Later, unable to sleep, she took up her usual vantage point in her kitchen, listening to the street and the world around it wind down. It was a habit that allowed her to take the night breeze in summer and warm herself by the stove in winter.

In her early eighties, she had lived in Collingwood with her husband far longer than most of the other locals and was entirely at home in this scrappy suburb on the edge of the city.

Like many of the terraced houses in the street, hers mirrored her neighbours'. But it was more basic; there was still a dirt floor in the kitchen, and a side fence of battered palings no more than three feet high. 'Old Collingwood', some neighbours would think as they passed. And so Gladys Coventry was, yet she was also perfectly attuned to the rhythms of the street and her 'twenty-something' neighbours.

She had seen many things during her decades in Easey Street. What she saw on this particular evening was never officially recorded, and has almost been lost to time.

A few doors up the street, Peter Sellers and a mate had settled in for the evening too, kicking back in front of the TV. The former apprentice jockey was savouring a little late-night freedom before his family returned from a sojourn interstate. What he and his friend heard, hours later, has also never been fully recorded or understood.

Three days later, some sixty hours after Martin Bartlett last saw his sister, as the city's temperature rose to nearly 33 degrees, Mrs Coventry watched as police swarmed on the cottage next door, and the covered bodies of the two young women were brought out on gurneys. They had been stabbed a collective eighty-four times.

Gladys Coventry saw the female police officer carry Gregory out of the house and into the waiting ambulance, headed for the children's hospital, as her neighbours huddled on the footpath across the street. It was summer holidays, so local youngster Phillip

Perez and his friends were there too, wheeling around on their bikes, not quite comprehending the grim scene unfolding or what to do within it.

Four decades later, five days after the fortieth anniversary of the double homicide that cast an indelible shadow on the city's soul, a million-dollar reward for new information was posted. But police are still to make an arrest. The killer is still free.

So a 42-year-old question stands, one that disturbs most who lived in Melbourne at the time, including steadfast young journalists: how can two women, not quite in the prime of their lives, die so violently at the hands of a man who just … vanishes?

The repeated refrain has been that no one saw or heard anything suspicious that night. Or the next night, or the one after that. But Easey Street tells a different tale of the week in January that forever changed the city. And Gladys Coventry could well be its true heart.

CHAPTER 1
THE MOVE

COLLINGWOOD PROBABLY WASN'T their first choice.

As inner-city suburbs went, it wasn't as trendy as Carlton, as hip as Fitzroy or as leafy as Clifton Hill. It was a rough-and-tumble little pocket on the edge of the city, with lines of unrenovated workers' cottages alternating with small factories, just a few minutes' walk from the Richmond housing commission flats.

But it was cheap, and that's likely the main reason 28-year-old Suzanne Armstrong was drawn to the small house she found in Easey Street to share with her friend, Susan Bartlett, and her young son, Gregory. Nothing fancy, it was neat and roomy enough for the now single mum, her son and her best friend to share comfortably. Her bike could even tuck in on the porch, just under the front window.

Not long back from Greece, where Greg had been born just over a year ago, Suzanne was keen to make a fresh start in Melbourne. And who better to do that with than her old ally Sue? The two had been friends ever since high school in Benalla, a country town in north-eastern Victoria. Bright, vibrant young women, they seemed to balance each other, each confident in their own way.

Suzanne had already spent time overseas, travelling through Asia, the United Kingdom and the United States between 1972 and 1973, on what, from her letters home, sounded like quite an adventure. She even admitted she had smuggled a suitcase of 'emeralds' that was really cocaine from Bogotá to Florida for two men she barely knew. Far from home and running low on travelling funds, the $400 they promised to pay for the illegal journey obviously appealed to her. But she never saw a dollar. 'I am so naive sometimes, I should be drawn and quartered,' she wrote to a friend. When she returned to Australia, Sue was in Greece. Suzanne began working as a taxi driver to save enough to be able to afford another trip and catch up with her mate, who had written to say what a great time she was having.

The pair reunited in August 1974 and cruised the Greek Islands together: Aegina, Delos, Hydra, Mykonos, Paros and eventually Naxos, where Suzanne met Manolis Margaritis, a handsome young fisherman. When Sue flew back to Australia in early 1975 to resume a teaching position at Collingwood Education Centre, Suzanne stayed on.

The reason for this was soon apparent. 'We've just been to Athens and I've seen a doctor there and he said I was definitely pregnant,' she wrote to her sister, Gayle, early in 1975.

> I am going to marry Manolis. I've decided it's the best thing to do. I know I won't lead the same sort of life I would if I was in Melbourne, but it will be a very simple life and I hope I will have all the comforts and conveniences I want.
>
> We won't be living here forever though. We'd better not,

> anyway … We have ordered our wedding rings; they are 14-carat yellow gold, with fine lines.

Romantic optimism started to fade a couple of months later. A prolific letter-writer, Suzanne confessed her concerns to Gayle as cultural differences became increasingly apparent, especially around her pregnancy. 'Boy, the things I get told not to do here, you wouldn't believe it,' she wrote. 'I'm not supposed to run an inch, not supposed to sit with my legs crossed or reach up or sit cross-legged on the bed (maybe they think the baby will fall out!) I'm not supposed to lift up Zebby [her dog] or lift anything, it's really incredible.'

Navigating an international maze of bureaucracy also proved disheartening; the documents required for Suzanne, so far from home, to marry a young Greek man proved impossible to organise, a futile pursuit. 'I don't know when we are going to get married,' she wrote in early May 1975. 'The priest here is such an old bum, and sometimes I don't know that I care all that much.'

The birth of their baby boy brought the couple joy, and Suzanne's mother, Eileen, was there to help with the new arrival. With her partner, Bruce Currie, she visited Naxos to welcome her grandson into the world, and her presence was a relief for her eldest daughter. But they couldn't stay on the island indefinitely, and an increasingly unhappy Suzanne realised that a decision loomed.

Leaving the island to return to Australia with her son, and without Manolis, was a huge step to take, far from an easy choice for any woman, especially for a new mother in 1975. Social mores were shifting, but raising a child alone still posed problems, and it must have been emotionally wrenching. Initially, perhaps to soften the blow, she told Manolis she would just be leaving temporarily, to celebrate Christmas with her family in December 1976. But this plan changed, she admitted in her last letter to her mother from Naxos. 'I know it will break his heart when I tell him I'm not coming back, but I will tell him then that the best thing is for him to come to Australia; if he makes it there, he will deserve another try. He keeps asking me if I am coming back and of course, I have to say yes. It's awful.'

Suzanne bought a one-way ticket home.

Even before leaving Greece, she must have realised that she needed support for this next major step in her life. She knew she could call on Sue for that support. It's probably safe to assume that her long-time friend wasn't surprised when Suzanne asked just a couple of months before Christmas in 1976 if she wanted to move in with the new mother and her son when they returned.

If Suzanne was somewhat impatient to forge a new path, Sue was revelling in teaching art and the strong circle of colleagues around her. Respected in her role as an arts and craft teacher at CEC, where she had been working for nearly five years, Sue loved the vibrancy of the inner-city high school and enjoyed the short drive from where she was living, in Richmond, with another friend. She drove a VW Beetle, and often dined in the city's Greek restaurants; long a fan of the cuisine, she was no doubt savouring her recent holiday on the Greek Islands. When her old schoolfriend reappeared in Melbourne with a baby boy, keen for her to share a place that was even closer to her school, Sue didn't seem to take much convincing to make the move, despite her mother's reservations. The two friends had gone to school together, come of age together, seen the world together; she and Suzanne clearly enjoyed each other's company, knew each other's history, and shared as a bedrock their upbringing in Benalla. She loved children, too, so her friend's toddler posed no problem.

While they had grown up in country Victoria, both women knew Melbourne well. Before travelling overseas in the mid-1970s, Suzanne had lived in South Yarra, then back across the river in inner-city Carlton, with its new 'alt theatre' scene at the Pram Factory and La Mama. While she was facing a struggle of sorts to re-establish herself in the city without a guaranteed income beyond her single mother's pension, she must have been eager to jump back into that world, as well as into the effervescence of Lygon and Brunswick streets.

As an old family friend recalls, it was an exciting time to be living in a big city, and the girls likely looked forward to making the most of it. For seven years, Gary Biddle lived next door to Sue, her mother and her brother in Mitchell Street, Benalla, and he has never forgotten the family. 'We got to know Martin very well, and Susan. When Mum and Dad used to go out, Susan would come and babysit us. I think she was about four years older than us – that was me, my twin brother and my sister. They were the most wonderful neighbours. She and Martin always had kind words to say, they never put anyone down.'

Gary has never forgotten Sue's passion for the new music of the era, especially a certain young band from Liverpool. 'Susan was a Beatles freak – she loved them. She went to their concert in Melbourne, I do remember that, at Festival Hall. She might even have gone with Suzanne.'

Sue's brother, Martin, confirms this trip, which the girls took down the Hume Highway. By bus. 'In those days there weren't a lot of bands, and the girls were in Benalla, and it was just one of those things; I mean, they were teenagers and The Beatles were just a phenomenon at the time.

'It was more their generation than mine. Even though there's only three years difference,' he says, mischievously, with a quick grin. A robust, handsome man now in his sixties, he loved his sister deeply. 'I was the Rolling Stones, which were just a bit later. I think I bought every Rolling Stones album. It was a bit of a hobby; import records from the UK when they were what they called "gold pressings" and stuff.'

Sue's love of music extended to live bands, which she went to see regularly while she was teaching at Broadford, before her move to Melbourne. Martin credits his mother, Elaine, as the cultural influence in their lives, noting her involvement with Benalla's local theatre and her genuine love of needlework and sewing. 'My mother and sister were both arty and crafty.'

To Gary, Sue epitomised the swinging sixties and effervescent seventies. 'I remember my mum going off one day about her,' he says with a laugh. 'She was wearing a miniskirt! Back in the early sixties, right?'

The stories tumble out, words a jumble, as he relives days as a youngster looking up to the girl next door. 'She was really what you'd call a trendsetter, because she was just with it. Finger-poppin' bubbly, just lovely,' he says, describing her 'Elizabeth Taylor–like' beauty and stylish dress sense. 'It's just something that stays with you. She was just with it, all the time.'

Gary remembers Suzanne Armstrong, too. 'Suzanne's [dress style] was more Flower Power. I can still picture her now, fifty years on. She was the kind of young woman every young man wanted to take out.'

It really didn't matter to Sue that her mother didn't like the idea of her moving in with Suzanne. Even though the girls were close, the two families were not. And mothers are mothers, after all. It's their inherent duty to worry about what their daughters do, who they spend time with and where they live.

So there was certainly discussion within the Bartlett family about the friends moving in together. Martin clearly recalls talking it over with his mother. 'Suzanne Armstrong had just come back from Greece and she was sort of like, "Oh, I don't know what's going to happen, because I've brought Greg back,"' he says. 'Obviously she's done a runner and she didn't know what the repercussions would be from the father of the child. So there was some sort of concern there from my mother and me; I mean, that's what we discussed.

'And look, Sue Armstrong was sort of pretty desperate to find a place and someone to share it with and my sister [was] probably more accommodating than most and she probably felt, "Oh, okay, I can help her out." So that's what she did.'

If Elaine Stanton Bartlett sensed that desperation in her daughter's friend, her concern would not have been eased by the girls' choice of suburb. 'Susan was living in The Crofts with another girl [when] Suzanne came back ... At the time, my mother said, "You're in a good spot in Richmond." It was just off Punt Road, opposite the MCG, and a nice house. I remember her saying, "Collingwood?" My sister said, "No, it seems to be a fairly quiet street." Which it was. But you know ...'

It was Collingwood.

And the 'runt end' of Collingwood at that, with major construction underway at one end of Easey Street as the already busy Hoddle Street was widened to feed into the new South-Eastern Freeway. If that wasn't disruptive enough, a health clinic was being built in the street behind them, its brick back wall bordering the yards of the first couple of houses in the street.

The history of the suburb was not salubrious. The area had been split in half in 1842 by surveyor Robert Hoddle and renamed 'Collingwood' and 'Fitzroy'. But east Collingwood, especially, dropped away to the boggy river flats that reached the Yarra. Some subdivision occurred on the higher ground, but 'Collingwood Flat' wasn't filled until the 1850s.

From the start, the suburb was dispatched to struggle. By 1861, some 13,000 residents had moved in. But just thirty years later Collingwood had the dubious distinction of recording the city's highest death rate – no doubt due to the 'noxious trades' for which it is still remembered. Tanneries sprung up next to brewers and brickmakers, providing employment for many semi-skilled and unskilled workers, who moved into the cheap housing built to accommodate them. Unions such as the Victorian Boot Operatives were born, and Collingwood resident Charles Jardine Don was elected as the state's first openly working-class MP in 1859.

When Collingwood Football Club kicked into action in the 1860s, it quickly became the heart and soul of the suburb. The hallowed playing ground remains significant today, its ardent benefactors following in the famous footsteps of John Wren, whose controversial career started with the illegal Collingwood Tote, a gambling venue that he ran from the back of a teashop on Johnston Street for more than a decade, from 1893.

Intriguingly, this social balance has always been one of Collingwood's most endearing traits, with various organisations set up to support the poor alongside the suburb's more salubrious elements. A free medical dispensary was opened in 1869 by Dr John Singleton and continued for an extraordinary 108 years, until its doors closed and the Collingwood Community Health Centre took over in 1977. Singleton is well known, too, for setting up a night shelter for women and a home for 'fallen women'. One of Australia's first creches also opened its doors in the 1880s, to assist mothers who worked locally.

Despite such a schizophrenic profile, Collingwood's council was keen to market itself as the 'premier suburban city in Melbourne'. Perhaps to back that claim, the rather ostentatious Collingwood Town Hall was built in 1886, smack bang in the middle of Hoddle Street.

For decades, it cast a positive shadow: some of the suburb's most dilapidated houses were torn down after the 1890s depression, and Foy & Gibson's department store moved in, just ahead of the new century. By then, Collingwood's Smith Street had become popular, the most important retail strip outside Melbourne's city centre, with business strong enough to support G.J. Coles opening its first variety store there in 1914. Trams carried passengers up and down the busy thoroughfares of Johnston, Smith and Victoria streets. Yet the ripple effect of the Wall Street crash of 1929 eventually reached Australia, and Collingwood felt its aftershocks particularly hard. Local employment dried up in the 1930s – and with widespread unemployment a national problem, the suburb again became a centre for cheap accommodation. Dirt cheap, it would seem. Historian Jill Barnard wrote, 'The pervading memory that many Collingwood residents had of the 1930s was the smell of "Collingwood Coke", burning leather offcuts collected from the dustbins of boot factories and used instead of wood.'

Ponch Hawkes, a prolific Australian photographer and artist, grew up in the suburb, on the southern side of Johnston Street. Her father worked in the laundry at the local convent for thirty-five years, and trained greyhounds as a hobby for most of his life. He would tell her about walking the dogs around Studley Park and bumping into John Wren, heading to town from his mansion, *Raheen*, which still overlooks the river from Studley Park Road in nearby Kew.

Ponch remembers Victoria Street before the Vietnamese families moved in and opened restaurants, turning the strip into one of Melbourne's key culinary destinations. More vividly, she recalls going to the grocer's as a child to buy broken biscuits. 'They'd sell you the biscuits that were left in the tin,' she says, juggling a hot chocolate in the Ladybird Café on the corner of Johnston and Wellington streets. 'You know, it was SP bookies [territory]. There was this underground gambling and betting activity kind of everywhere. And it was an area where people knew everybody. You knew that person, and they knew that person. Of course, I'm looking back on it now, [but] as a kid, it was normal. It's just what it was. It had no "side", you know what I mean? There were no fancy shops or nothing that you'd imagine any middle-class person going into or anything.'

And when the locals had a night on the town, they stayed local. 'If you went out with your parents, it was going to the dogs or going coursing, or going to visit their friends. If we went to play ourselves, [it was] Studley Park, we went there all the time. And my brother went to Collingwood Tech.'

Ponch Hawkes left the house her parents had lived in 'for a million years' when she went to Monash University in 1964. And slowly, as this nascent photographer started capturing all that was happening at the Pram Factory in Carlton and helped set up Circus Oz just around the corner, her old stomping ground started to change shape.

The little inner-city pocket bounced back. Again. This time with the unexpected influx of migrants, who also found the cheap housing appealing. By 1971, overseas-born residents comprised more than 40 per cent of the population, and with several generations of that Greek, Italian and Indo-Chinese infusion, Collingwood has never looked back.

Over the next two decades, whole blocks of houses were razed and replaced by medium- and high-rise flats, the widening of Hoddle Street and the construction of the F19 Freeway (now known as the Eastern Freeway) to Doncaster placing a physical divide between Collingwood and neighbouring Clifton Hill. University students and middle-class professionals eventually noticed how handy the area was in terms of transport, how big some of the blocks were, how the historic buildings added grace and history to the surrounds and how much impact fledgling radio stations 3CR and 3RRR were having from their knockabout studios in Collingwood and Carlton. Workers' cottages were renovated for the first of many times, old warehouses transformed.

Such was the air of reinvention that American artist Keith Haring visited the neighbourhood in 1984, gracing the free-standing side of Collingwood Tech with one of his renowned 'dancing man' street murals.

Beyond Smith Street, Fitzroy now beckoned. But only for hardier souls. 'I had my [photographic] studio there for fourteen years, and I remember some people at the Pram Factory had this idea of buying a row of four terraces in the street beside it,' Ponch Hawkes recalls. 'And they were terraces that came right into the street. I just said, "They're slums." That [was like] going back to the slums to me. Of course, you'd be a millionaire if you owned them now.'

When Suzanne Armstrong and Sue Bartlett moved into the suburb right next door to Fitzroy in late 1977, they must have sensed they were on the cusp of Collingwood's reawakening, its second act.

They loved the area. There was a milk bar on the corner, a good bus service, a couple of hospitals nearby – and the rent was affordable, maybe half of what some were paying in Carlton. Suzanne posted the $100 bond and the pair moved into the three-bedroom cottage in mid-October 1976.

The house was simple but comfortable, boasting the layout of so many inner-city rentals at the time, with three rooms running off the hallway to the right and a small lounge room at the end, the kitchen and bathroom at the back of the house. House-sharing was the 'new norm', the way thousands of young Australians were living in cities around the country, sharing rent and food and household chores, within the shifting cultural landscape.

The girls settled in quickly, Suzanne choosing the front bedroom, with a window that looked out over the front porch and onto the street, and Sue taking the third, with a window that opened to the side laneway. Gregory's cot was in the room between them, also used as a sewing space.

They set up a couch, a television and a stereo system in the small living room. The phone hung near the door that opened to the hall. The compact kitchen was brimming with energy too, little Greg's painted wooden highchair under open shelves lined with travellers' trinkets; a couple of ceramic jugs sat above a mounted snow globe and a seashell that had perhaps jetted in from a Greek Island beach.

Off to the side of the kitchen was the narrow bathroom, a large floral mat matching the carnations and roses adorning the shower curtain hanging in the bath.

Outside, the yard, with its thatch of grass and Hills Hoist, meant that Mishka, the fourth member of this new family – a cheerful young dog with a long white blaze over her left eye – was well catered for, her kennel tucked under the kitchen window for outside shelter.

So it wasn't fancy, but it was a home, and from all accounts a cheerful one that those who visited felt welcome in.

As Melbourne's wet spring edged towards summer, the girls had a quiet housewarming and, several weeks later, with Christmas holidays in full swing, Susan Bartlett's teaching colleagues made up the numbers at their New Year's Eve party. They had a barbeque going in the backyard and music playing. Maybe Chicago X was on the stereo; Pete Cetera's short, lovelorn ballad 'If You Leave Me Now' was a central part of that summer's tapestry. That is, unless the hosts were into local groups like Skyhooks and Jo Jo Zep and The Falcons. It was an explosive time for inner-city music, with indie punk groups Bleeding Hearts and Stiletto on the ascendency. But whatever they were dancing to, friends there that night describe two happy young women embracing the crackle of change in the air and the community around them. It was invigorating.

Su-lin Loh remembers Sue as a powerful presence in her family's life. Sue was friends with her mother, Morag Loh, an academic and co-author of *The Immigrants*, and the Lohs would stay with the Bartletts at their beach house at Inverloch. Sometimes Nick Dimopoulis, Sue's boyfriend, would be with her. 'When she and Nick came to the beach, they just slotted in and were really nice to be around; he was Greek and terribly proper, a gentleman.'

Su-lin also met Suzanne Armstrong at the Easey Street housewarming. She left quite an impression on the teenager. 'I only met her once, but I remember it really clearly. Suzanne had on a pair of white trousers and a green extended boob tube. She had beautiful hair, very seventies hair.' She laughs. 'And I remember thinking, "You're beautiful and you look amazing." She just seemed like a lovely person too.

'My memory of them both is that they were happy, confident, friendly, outgoing – and enjoying life. Sue Bartlett was just brimming with confidence. She wasn't a small girl, but she was completely comfortable in her own skin and how she looked. She was a good teacher too, she was respected at work.

'They were girls of their time, very much so. But they weren't wild "party girls". They were nice, really nice. If they had a few boyfriends and had a party, I just think good on them.'

Martin Bartlett was at the house for both gatherings and recalls a pleasant, low-key affair on New Year's Eve, a gentle, unassuming welcoming-in of the year ahead. 'Every time I went over there, there weren't people knocking on the door, or dropping in or phoning and saying, "Hey, can I come over?" or "Are you going to do this?" I mean, very quiet, very quiet. It was not a party [lifestyle].'

His sister was looking forward to consolidating the career she so loved, and enjoying a friendly, if casual, relationship with a young salesman, successful enough to have purchased a white Mercedes, which he occasionally parked in Easey Street. Well and truly standing out. For Suzanne, too, the start of the new year must have felt like a positive point.

Keen to reshape her life in Australia with her young son, she had reunited with her family – especially Gayle, the oldest of her two younger sisters, who had a son just two weeks older than Gregory. A few days after the New Year's Eve gathering at Easey Street, in fact, Suzanne went on a blind date with the brother of Gayle's boyfriend. They hit it off, and went out twice more, each time with her toddler in tow, culminating in Sunday-afternoon lunch at his sister's house a couple of suburbs away. They took the portable television outside and sat on the lawn with his family, and made plans to have dinner together two nights later.

Her new beau took her home that Sunday night, 9 January 1977. He met Susan over a cup of tea, and her friend, who'd parked his car out the front. As he left, he promised to call Suzanne the next day.

And he did. Many times.

But no one answered.

CHAPTER 2

THE MURDERS

ON THE LAST day of her life, Sue Bartlett spent time with her family. In the morning, she met her mother, and they did what mothers and daughters so often do together – they went shopping. They even visited the salubrious Georges department store, where they had lunch, quite a special outing in Melbourne at the time.

Returning home in the afternoon, Sue worked on a dress she was making, putting the relaxed summer Monday to good use. Hours later, she made dinner for her brother, Martin, who was three years younger. They were good friends, as well as siblings. She could call on him for all kinds of things. That night, she had a specific chore in mind: fixing her stereo.

'I went over to do that. And I got it going,' he says. 'Women are not that practical with stuff like that, but I was always tinkering with Meccano sets and things. So I knew what to do.'

He took his girlfriend, Vicki Crowe, with him and they stayed for a couple of hours, having dinner with Sue and Suzanne before he took to his task in earnest. So that he could hear as well as see what he was doing to fix the stereo system, the television was turned off between 8.00 and 8.25 pm.

As Martin tinkered, the phone rang. 'My sister answered it, but the call was for Suzanne ... my sister called out to her that she was wanted on the phone. Suzanne came to the telephone ... and the stereo was turned down low. I think she said, "It's Loretta," [and] when Suzanne was on the phone, I heard her say, "Sue's brother Martin and a friend."'

Suzanne and the caller he presumed was her sister, Loretta Armstrong, spoke between 8.15 and 8.20 pm. Not much later, the women decided to watch television. 'I was about to put the other side of the record on when the girls said that they wanted to watch *The Sullivans*.' Suzanne was just going to put Gregory to bed first.

Martin and Vicki decided to visit a friend of hers in Glen Waverley, but before they departed Martin made a date with his sister to come back for dinner in about a week's time. As the couple left at around 9.00 pm, Sue and her friend were settled in front of the television.

No one knows what happened in the house beyond this point except the killer. Based on what's known of the girls' habits and of the crime scene police discovered, it may have unfolded like this.

With her son sleeping soundly in his small bedroom, Suzanne could relax and enjoy the period drama she and Susan watched regularly. For many Australians, *The Sullivans* was a reassuring treat – a fictional soap opera set in a touchstone era for older viewers, while younger fans marvelled at that great divide: then and now.

When it finished, the friends might have shared another cup of tea before retiring to different ends of the house – Suzanne to settle down with the book of short stories she had started, Sue perhaps keen to have another look at the dress she had been working on earlier in the day.

Maybe she thought she could do some washing before it got too late. The washing machine was in the bathroom, just off the kitchen, far enough away from the bedrooms not to wake Greg or to bother Suzanne, whose room was even further up the corridor. Sue probably closed the door to the corridor, too, to muffle any noise.

She might have sorted through some clothes and loaded them into the washing machine out in the back of the house. If so, she wouldn't have heard a *tap, tap, tap* on the front door, or a quiet murmur of voices as Suzanne opened it. Or perhaps the visitor opened the front window and jumped in that way, which would have been even harder to hear from the other end of the house.

Far enough away to not sense anything wrong, Sue most likely hovered, tidying up the kitchen, maybe sitting outside in the cool night air and playing with Mishka as she checked the side gate was closed to keep the puppy safe. Her brother is sure she would have locked the back door behind her when she returned inside. The women might have hailed from the country, where security did not invoke the same degree of attention as in inner-city Melbourne, but she and Suzanne were careful. For Greg's sake, even more than for their own.

And then, perhaps she was ready for bed ... did she hear something odd from the front of the house? A thump, perhaps, as if something or someone had fallen. Either way, Sue would have walked through the kitchen and the small lounge room, opening the door into the hallway, quickly passing her own room.

If she had looked into Greg's room, she would have seen him safely in his cot, hopefully asleep. But there, again ... was there a noise, still muffled but closer now, more distinct? Perhaps Sue had a strong sense that something wasn't right as she walked further towards the front of the house.

And suddenly, she would have seen *him*, perhaps stepping back from behind the door in Suzanne's room and looking up from the floor. Then he was in the passageway. Was he as stunned to see her as she was him?

Armed with a knife, he lunged. The first cuts sliced her arms, hands and neck, as she faced her attacker, fighting back. The knife wounds found on her hands indicate that she punched at him as the knife slashed her, and at some stage, as she tried to weave away from the assault, she must have seen Suzanne lying on her bedroom floor. For a second or two, at least, confusion surely mingled with physical pain, and rising panic. Why didn't Suzanne get up to help her, Sue might have wondered as she tried to dodge that knife again, the intruder coming after her with even greater force. Couldn't she hear what was happening? Had he wounded Suzanne so badly she could not come to her aid? Perhaps she realised her friend was already dead.

Sue had no way of knowing the fight her friend had waged, grabbing the knife with her hands and trying to push it away, sustaining a deep gash in the process, before it was thrust into her chest. Then twice more. Stopping her there, on her bedroom floor.

In the hallway, it seems Sue turned and tried to reach the front door, making a lunge for it, her hands bloodied. The knife stabbed her in the back this time, and then her legs, penetrating over and again, as she fell to her knees and the attacker forced her back down the hall. Away from the front door. Away from her friend.

He stabbed Sue in a frenzy. Did she will herself to lie there, as still as possible, so perhaps his rage would dissipate and he would leave her alone? If she was left bleeding on the floor in the middle of the dark hall, she might still have been able to inch her way back to the front door. And get help.

Sue Bartlett died just metres away from the front door, close to Suzanne Armstrong, who was still on the floor just behind her bedroom door.

The women sustained eighty-two stab wounds between them. But the assailant continued his attack. Police believe he raped the prostrate body of Suzanne, the woman most investigators who have studied this case believe he came to see that night.

At least one says there are indications that the murderer took his time arranging Suzanne's body, perhaps even wiping the blood from her wounds before he walked to the back of the house to clean the blood off himself. Off his hands, his arms, his face, his clothes. All while the sixteen-month-old infant lay in his cot a room away.

Then the killer walked out the back door and into the quiet summer night.

CHAPTER 3

THE NEIGHBOURS

WHEN ILONA STEVENS woke up on Tuesday 11 January, she quickly got dressed, made a cup of tea and agreed, without much coaxing, to drive her colleague John Grant home.

The journalist had slept on the couch in the lounge room of the house she shared with her friend Janet Powell, who ran the Italian restaurant Casanova in Carlton. After a few drinks at the Celtic Club in the city, Ilona and Grant had arrived back at Collingwood at about 8.15 pm. They played pool and drank together until Janet got home just after midnight. The three stayed up talking until about 2.00 am. Given the late hour, Ilona made up the couch for him before going to bed herself.

Nicknamed 'Grunter', John Grant was an old-fashioned crime reporter who worked both sides of his 'beat', with as many criminal sources as police contacts in his notebooks. His reputation as a hard drinker preceded him – and so too his connection with a tragedy that had occurred two years earlier.

Grant was one of the last people known to have been with Julie Ann Garciacelay before she disappeared in 1975. She has not been seen since, has not contacted friends or family, but nor has her body been found. He was at the time a 'person of interest' in the missing person's investigation. His fellow workers at *Truth*, a Murdoch tabloid, were aware of this, but Grant swore that he had nothing to do with the nineteen-year-old American vanishing.

Grant's connection to the girl's disappearance troubled some of his colleagues, but not Ilona. She enjoyed his company and felt sorry for the beleaguered reporter; it was another reason to be kind to him, especially after he confided that his father, with whom he lived, was an alcoholic and physically abusive.

When she awoke that Tuesday, Grant was already up, showered and ready to leave. As she roused him out towards her car just before 8.00 am, she thought she could hear young Gregory crying next door. This struck her as odd, because he rarely cried for long at all; Suzanne Armstrong was an attentive mother.

Her neighbours hadn't lived next door long, moving in two months before Christmas 1976, so she didn't know them well. But Suzanne was a single mum who clearly loved her son, zipping round the neighbourhood with him on the back of her bike, and nicking over to the corner milk bar with him on her hip. Her friend Sue, who shared the cottage, also seemed at ease with the toddler, a willing support to Suzanne.

Even happy kids cry, Ilona reasoned, so she didn't give Greg much more thought that Tuesday morning. But later that day, when she returned from work, another odd thing occurred. Her house-mate, Janet, asked if the women living next door – the 'two Sues', as they called them – had a puppy. When dog-loving Ilona confirmed this, her friend told her that she had just seen a young dog running loose on the street.

Janet enticed the dog into their house. Eventually, they went next door to let their neighbours know they had the naughty pup, a cheerful German Shepherd cross. 'We both went to the front door of 147 Easey Street with the puppy. We knocked a couple of times, but there was no answer. We then took the puppy back into our house and put it in the backyard,' Ilona later told police.

This didn't seem overly concerning to either Ilona or Janet. The girls had probably been in and out all day, and the dog had managed to evade being 'recaptured', they thought. At least now she was safe at their place.

Ilona went out for dinner with friends in South Yarra. When she got home, the dog was still there, despite Janet's efforts to raise their neighbours a couple of times during the evening. This now seemed a bit strange and, late as it was, Ilona decided to take matters in hand. She went into her backyard and shouted over the fence, but was unable to raise anyone. Getting on a chair, she looked over and saw the back door open and a light on. Yet there was still no response to her calls.

Tired as they were, Ilona and Janet decided to try another tack: they'd write a note about the pup and leave it on the girls' front door. At about 11.30 pm, the two friends pinned a piece of paper on the door. *Dear Sue's* [sic], it read. *We have your dog which was wandering around the street. You are obviously not home. So give us a yell and we will return same to you PROMPTLY. Regards, Ilona and Janet.*

Back at home, Ilona had a bath and heard the phone ringing next door. 'I heard the phone ring in 147 and it rang itself out. This happened a couple of times. I then went to bed. Again, I heard nothing unusual during the night.'

She went to work again the next morning, not noticing that the note was still on her neighbours' door until she got back later that night. Neither Sue nor Suzanne had dropped in to pick up the dog, and Ilona could hear Greg crying, if intermittently. In fact, she recalls hearing the little boy crying, on and off, over these two days, just as his puppy barked and barked in her backyard.

Janet also saw that the light was still on in their neighbours' house when she arrived home later that Wednesday night, and for the first time she felt frightened. 'At this stage, I felt that there was something wrong.'

Ilona was already asleep, so they didn't discuss it again until the next morning. By now, both women were alarmed. What was going on next door?

'The dog's still running around and the baby's still crying, but stopping – you know, getting quieter, which kind of rang alarm bells. It was just not like them to let him cry ... [but] it was getting quieter and quieter. It was weak crying.

'You could still hear it through the wall, but you could hear breathing through those walls. They were single-brick, just a single party wall, so you could hear [him] – and that's what concerned me. If he'd cried normally, I would have gone, "Oh yes, he's been fed and looked after," but he was crying weakly.'

The two walked out their little front gate and in through the gate of 147 Easey Street. This time there would be no turning back until they raised the 'two Sues'. Ilona went to the door and knocked loudly. No response. She banged on it again, harder. Nothing.

'So I said to Janet, "Well, I'll go over the fence, just make sure everything's OK."'

Here, talking about it forty years on, her memory diverges from what is recorded in the women's police interviews, in which they both say they entered the property through the side gate on the lane and stepped into the kitchen together. As Ilona remembers it now, she clambered over the fence that separated the backyards of 149 and 147 and walked in through their neighbours' back door, calling out as she entered.

But what happened next, she can never forget. 'I looked straight through the house. I could see Susan's feet, right at the very end of the corridor.'

With no lights on in the hall, and the only windows on the far side of the bedrooms, which were to the left of where she was standing, Ilona says the hallway was quite dimly lit. Even so, she could make out the feet clearly. 'I saw her feet ... and I didn't look anywhere else. I went straight down the hall and I just remember as I got to her, her feet were black. From being there and not moving, I guess.'

It was clear that the 27-year-old was dead. As Ilona bent over Sue, whose body was lying face down and close to the front door, she glanced into the front bedroom and saw Suzanne's body.

At that point, she realised she had not seen Gregory.

'I saw her and then I back-tracked,' Ilona says. 'He was still doing [those] weak little cries.' As she walked carefully into his room, she could see that he wasn't in good shape. He looked weak, dehydrated. And even as Ilona hovered over him, he just lay there in his cot.

She spoke to him gently, trying to reassure him that help was coming. But she didn't reach in and pick him up. 'I wasn't going to lift him up and try to comfort him, because this was not good!'

She's adamant about this, despite her police statement saying she picked Greg up and took him back to her house. 'That didn't happen, so I don't know why they've written it up like that. I don't remember the detective who took my statement taking many notes; maybe that's what he thought I did. But there's no way I did that. I had no experience with babies, especially a young child who was clearly distressed. He needed help that I couldn't give him, and I didn't want to make things any worse than they already were.'

Instead, she sang out to her housemate, who was waiting anxiously on the other side of the fence. 'I called out to Janet, "Ring the police, they're dead."

'She ran inside, picked up the black phone, dialled – and it took them forever to come. I reckon it took a good twenty minutes.'

Her friend had to call a second time, in fact, to convince police they were needed in Easey Street. 'They sort of went, "Yeah … what?" I suppose some girl rings them up and says, "My neighbours are dead, my flatmate's in there …" They kept questioning her, and she got shitty. Then they sent one car, with one young guy. They didn't even send two [police officers]. One, that's all.'

By the time the officer arrived, Janet had walked around the side of the house, in through the gate, and looked up the hallway and seen Sue Bartlett's body. But Ilona stopped her from going inside the house. 'She's not like me, and I didn't want her to see what I had just seen. I wanted to protect her from that.' Both women were well aware, too, that their neighbours' house was now a crime scene.

With Sue Bartlett's body lying almost at the front door in the narrow hall, Ilona also realised she had to stop the police officer from trying to enter the house that way. So she hurried out the side gate and into the short laneway to meet the young officer as he was knocking at the door.

'Susan was right there, so you couldn't have opened it. I do recall being in the lane talking to this young guy and he's going, "What's going on here?"

'Hello, I thought, took you long enough to get here.

'I said, "You're obviously not taking this seriously! They're dead." He went inside and looked – and the next thing, there were twenty cars and men in suits.'

A young policewoman also arrived, to place the toddler in a waiting ambulance. As they watched him being taken away, the detectives realised they had a great deal of work ahead of them. There were two dead bodies to attend to, and a house to comb for evidence.

Some things were immediately obvious. For one, the killer had not rushed away after attacking the women. He had clearly felt safe enough to try to clean himself up before leaving. The bathroom was a mess, with bloodstains on the bath suggesting he had stood in it and tried to wash himself down, if not take a shower; there was some evidence of blood in the sink. It seemed, too, the killer even had the presence of mind to think about using the washing machine, as there was blood on its lid.

Ilona struggled to come to terms with the blood she had seen in the hall, where it looked as if Sue Bartlett had tried to pull herself closer to the front door.

Months later, a senior police officer would tell Ilona that Sue might still have been alive at the time of her first visit. 'She had some huge amount of stab wounds … but apparently they didn't hit anything vital and so she was trying to get to the front door, because I was banging on the other side. So how good do I feel?'

A direct, intelligent woman now in her sixties, Ilona refuses to overplay her role in this case, or her unusually consistent recall of what she discovered that awful morning. She will not place herself at the centre of the tragedy, or use words such as 'haunted' or 'disturbed' to describe how she felt after finding the women's bodies. Yet that detective's comment has stayed with her for forty years.

Criminologists who have looked at the crime scene photographs in the last year as part of the research for this book believe that the senior officer's theory could not have been correct. Sue had been stabbed so many times she would not have been able to move much, if at all.

Perhaps this perspective will bring Ilona some comfort.

CHAPTER 4

THE DETECTIVES

ONE OF THE first detectives to arrive at the scene wasn't much older than the two women whose lives, and deaths, he would come to know intimately.

Detective Senior Constable Peter Hiscock was thirty years old that January when he arrived at 147 Easey Street. Right from the start, he and the team from Victoria's Homicide Squad seemed on the back foot. For one thing, the young detective didn't think he was attending a murder, let alone two.

It wasn't what he and his team had expected to find when they got the call to attend the house. They thought they were attending a murder–suicide. 'Because there were two of them. We thought it might have been a fight between them, we didn't know,' he recalls. 'That's how it sort of came across. So [it was] one of those ones [where] we'd go down there and have a look at it, then ring up Collingwood CIB and say, "Look here, guys, you do the inquest brief."'

As he scanned the front gate and verandah, and saw the bike with the baby seat strapped on leaning against the front wall, he was directed to enter through the back door. Immediately, he knew the police assumption about what had happened in the little house was wrong 'and quickly, quickly, quickly assessed that this was a murder. Double murder, very serious murder. We were the first ones in there. It was just harrowing.'

Peter Hiscock suddenly found himself at the centre of a crime of heartbreaking horror. The young detective switched into 'professional mode' as he examined the two women lying dead on the floor of their inner-city home. 'You don't think about yourself, or anything like that. No, no, no. I know this sounds hard, [but] in actual fact we're taught by the pathologist that they're exhibits. That's what we're looking at, and they can tell us a lot of information.'

The crime scene was secured, with the young uniformed officer who had been first to arrive now officially guarding the property. 'Then it was a matter of getting as many available detectives from Homicide and [other] areas to come down and help us.'

At the time, police protocol did not dictate that they wait for the forensic team to arrive to maintain the integrity of the crime scene, or that they wear protective clothing or footwear. The detectives moved through the house together, becoming increasingly aware that this was an unusually frenzied attack. Both women had been stabbed many, many times over – there were too many wounds to estimate their number at this stage. Working their way from the backyard to the front bedroom, the police carefully noted the layout of the single-fronted brick terrace.

Like everyone else arriving at the property, the lead detective, Detective Senior Sergeant Alf Oldfield, walked in from the lane, noticing as he did that the second window on the side of the house was slightly open. Entering the yard through the side gate, he made his way into the kitchen. As he glanced around the room, a square of paper under an ashtray on the kitchen bench caught his eye. A note, short and to the point. *Barry Woodard*, it read. *RING 4803932 NOW. Barry*. A couple of arrows drew attention to the phone number and the signature.

Oldfield moved on, making his way further inside, passing the bathroom off to the right of the kitchen, the blood smear on the bath clearly visible. In the lounge room, he saw a bloodied towel on the couch, before he finally reached the hallway, where Sue Bartlett lay. As he made his way towards her body, he noticed a sandal and two plastic spray-can tops lying along the passageway.

He headed towards the front of the house, and glanced into the bedrooms on his left. Sue's was the first he reached, and he saw that the blind had fallen away from the window. He took a closer look. 'On the bedspread near the window was what appeared to be a footprint in dirt. Apart from this, the room did not appear to be untidy. The [next] room contained a cot, single bed, small table with a sewing machine on it.'

Back in the hall, he took a few more steps to finally reach Sue, lying at the door of the front room. She was face down, on her stomach, arms by her side. So very close to the front door, and her friend just metres away in the front bedroom. On the walls either side of her body were bloody spots and smears. He could see 'several stab wounds on the body'.

Closer examination, of course, would prove this to be a massive understatement. But Alf Oldfield and Peter Hiscock were reporting on their initial inspection.

He gingerly inched past Sue's body to look in around the bedroom door. There, Detective Oldfield saw Suzanne lying on her back. Her legs were wide apart, her nightdress pulled up over her breasts, where she had been stabbed. A vase of dried flowers had been knocked over and was lying on its side to the left of her body, and just above her head the carpet appeared to be bloodstained. On the floor at the bottom of the bed, there were more signs of busy, happy lives, now lost: a reel of black cotton, a toy telephone, a shopping bag and a pair of white towelling shorts.

The veteran investigator steadied himself as he glanced around the room, taking in as many details as he could. He knew they would reveal much about what had happened to the woman lying on the floor in front of him. At the same time, he realised the disparities of the grim scene. While Suzanne's sheets had been 'neatly pulled aside', there appeared to be small spots of blood on the top sheet, and a smear of blood on the bottom. A book had been placed at the top of the bed, face down and still open, but a pair of 'ladies panties' lay on the floor at the left side of the bed. The contrasts were chilling.

By the time the whole investigative team arrived – two officers from the forensic science laboratory, along with a fingerprint expert and a police photographer – a theory was forming in Alf Oldfield's mind.

Strange as it was, he could see that the violence of the stabbings the 'two Sues' had endured was not reflected in their immediate surroundings. There were few signs that a major struggle had taken place. The attacker had apparently entered the house through the front door, either opening it himself, or possibly having it opened by Suzanne Armstrong. The women had gone to bed, police surmised that first morning in the bloodsoaked house, when someone had arrived on the front porch and knocked at the door, or maybe tapped quietly on the front window to get Suzanne's attention. Even though at least four people would report the side gate and back door being open, and someone had left a note in the kitchen, suggesting that the attacker could have come in the back from the lane, the theory that the killer came in through the front of the house is what the first detectives on the scene believed. And the hypothesis is still given merit, nearly two generations later.

As the temperature started to rise that summer morning of 13 January 1977, the pieces began to come together for Peter Hiscock, too. Alf Oldfield's theory fit with what the young detective had encountered upon entering the house. The attacker would have seen the light on in the front room, he reasoned, because Suzanne was more than likely still up and reading Roald Dahl's *Switch Bitch* in bed, a collection of short stories that was opened halfway through 'The Last Act' when Hiscock entered the room. This suggested she had left her bed calmly, perhaps to go to the door. 'I clearly remember the bed. The sheet was just one fold back, and the book was on the side table. So … she knew the person. She put the book down, she didn't chuck it and kick the sheets away with her legs [to get] out of the bed.'

Alternatively, the murderer walked into the house himself. 'The front door wasn't locked, so someone's come in. It was closed, but not locked. Things weren't that bad back then. There was no forced entry. He's got through the door and she's seen him.'

There are a number of possible scenarios, of course. Perhaps he knocked on the front door and Suzanne let him in; he might have spoken to her, quietly, through the front window, asking to see her – and then she opened the door. Then again, he might have tapped on the window and slipped in that way, to make as little noise as possible. There were no security bars to prevent that happening.

Either way, 'I would think she knew him, and I believe there's only one person, and he has hit her with the knife because she's recognised him. There would have been a big commotion, a bit of a fight before he finally gets her to the ground,' the former detective surmises when we discuss the case, four decades on.

'Susan Bartlett, in the other room, hears this and has come up the passageway. She's a bigger-framed girl, and she's put up a fair fight, we think, because these defensive wounds, they've gone through to the bone.'

Hiscock is now a private investigator. A wiry, active man in his early seventies, his steely blue eyes are complemented by his grey hair. Over the course of his career he has investigated many cases, but this is the one that confounds him. Even after so much time, some things are hard to comprehend.

In a final act of degradation, the attacker 'interfered' with Suzanne Armstrong's body. 'That is gruesome. Necrophilia is what it's called, and it's probably the worst thing you can even think about,' he says, his voice faltering.

He stares into the distance for several seconds. 'Her legs were [spread] and he'd had sex with her after she was dead ... it's happened in hospitals, it's happened in mortuaries, but I don't know of any other cases where you see this out in a murder scene.'

Having inspected the bodies, the detectives worked their way back down the hallway, careful not to touch the blood-spattered walls on either side. Inexplicably, given the amount spilled in the attacks, there were no bloodied footprints to follow.

They again passed the second and third bedrooms, noting that while the footprint on Sue's bedspread had dirt on it, no blood seemed to have been spilled in her room.

The bathroom was another matter. It was awash with physical evidence of the terrible violence that had occurred in the little house days earlier. Someone smeared with blood had washed their hands in the sink and perhaps even stood in the bath to try to wash themselves down.

At the time, the investigative techniques police had at their disposal were limited to blood grouping and fingerprints. There was no DNA testing available to forensically match the evidence so plainly on view in the house – on the bodies, the walls, the floors and especially in the bathroom. But this didn't stop these 'first responders' from trying to extract as much physical information as they could, as quickly as possible. Peter Hiscock remembers getting down on his hands and knees with colleagues, all of them dressed in suits, ties and leather shoes, and pulling up the drain to check if anything of significance had collected there.

They found bone splinters.

'He must have been covered in blood,' Hiscock muses. 'He had a shower to wash [it] off, and we did something really unusual for the time. We took up the pipes in the bathroom and in the "elbow" [of the drain] there was little splinters of bone that were on the knife.'

The detectives believed this proved the killer knew something about their investigative procedures, as he clearly understood how important it was to wash away as much evidence as he could of his brutal attack. 'So he'd washed it all down, and washed himself down – and that could be somebody who knows investigative techniques. They had to know to [do that]; that stuff was pretty new. So someone knew something.'

Then again, he might simply have wanted to clean himself up before leaving the house.

That wasn't all that was waiting to be discovered in the house. The team returned to the kitchen bench, where the short note was pinned under the ashtray. The police read it carefully. Who was Barry? When had he left the note, and which of the two women was it for? Had he entered the house through the back gate, and if so been the one to leave it open? And if he had been in the kitchen after the women's deaths, why hadn't he called police straight away?

In Hiscock's mind, there was no way anyone could have innocently come through that door after the women had been killed and not seen their bodies. Whether they came through the back door or clambered in the side window, the house was too small, the layout too tight, for them not to glance up the passageway and see Sue Bartlett's body, or hear Greg Armstrong's cries. It beggared belief.

'I mean, it's human nature; you're going to look around. "I've been trying to ring these girls, I want to get hold of them" – and you're not going to see if they're there? I doubt it.'

And the little boy was in the house too, alone in his cot. 'Whether he was whimpering or whatever, we won't ever know. But he'd certainly had no food, no drink, he had nothing, his nappy was soiled ... Human nature [says] you'd look around.'

As the number of detectives working their way through the murder scene grew, the young detective accompanied the two bodies to the city morgue, driving behind the government undertaker's van. He also has a graphic memory of counting the stab wounds they had each sustained, marking their specific placement on two official diagrams that became part of the case file. 'I remember getting so close to them and pointing to them [the wounds] with my pen, making sure I didn't miss anything,' he recalls. 'I didn't want to miss anything, after all they'd gone through.'

Like many investigators, Hiscock believes the first forty-eight hours in any murder investigation 'are the most important – they can make or break your case'. At this early stage of inquiry, the detectives thought this would be an easy case. 'We thought we were going to solve this pretty quickly,' he admits. At the very least, there was blood they could test, fingerprints to collect, a note with a phone number to follow up and a footprint to trace.

Hiscock didn't stay on the case beyond the first few weeks of 1977, because he was scheduled to take annual leave, yet he recalls the confidence the Homicide Squad had. 'Such a violent crime for the time, you think, "It's going to be easy to solve."'

To start with, they would locate the 'Barry' who had left his number on the scrap of paper under the ashtray in the kitchen and determine exactly how he fitted into this grim puzzle.

Within days, the reporters gathering on the footpath outside 147 Easey Street would help to reveal not only who Barry was, but also how important Suzanne Armstrong was to him.

By then, police were already focusing on another suspect – a young man for whom ominous coincidence would prove unforgiving for the rest of his life.

CHAPTER 5
THE EXAMINERS

As the Homicide detectives left the house to start their inquiries, the team from the Forensic Science Laboratory were just beginning their work inside.

A small unit from the field investigation division had been dispatched to 147 Easey Street not long after police arrived at the scene, and Sergeant Henry Huggins carefully entered the house through the front door, quickly inspecting the bodies that lay in the hallway and front bedroom. He then went to the back of the property, where he was joined by Moira McBain, a chemist with the laboratory. It was the first time the crime-scene examiner had managed to persuade the forensics lab to allow a chemist to accompany him to a murder site.

As the pair started their slow, very particular search of the house, a detective handed Huggins a bloodstained towel, which was quickly bagged as evidence.

Under Huggins' meticulous direction, McBain examined all bloodstained areas deemed significant. She also collected samples that would be labelled and listed by a police constable assigned to work with them.

Collecting evidence from a crime scene is dry, almost clinical work that requires fastidious observation and precise reporting. Henry Huggins was up to the challenge. A third of the way into a career as an examiner that would span twenty-six years, he was used to difficult scenarios, and what he found that morning at 147 Easey Street shone light on how the double homicide unfolded – and what happened in the house as the women lay dead on the floor. The killer didn't rush away; that was as obvious to the forensics team as it had been to the police.

In the kitchen, the light was on. 'The sink was dry, the stove was turned off and the kettle on the stove was dry,' Huggins wrote in his report. 'There was a piece of paper on the corner bench. It had the words *Barry Woodard 4803932* ... there were a number of fibres on the high chair.'

Huggins saw three pages of newsprint on the floor – pages fifteen to eighteen of *The Age* newspaper dated 13 January 1977 – and was handed the first ten pages of the same edition by a detective. How did the three pages on the floor get there? It was a niggling question he left to his colleagues to answer as he continued his search of the house. They eventually surmised that the young police officer had brought it inside.

The light was on in the bathroom, too. 'The three-pin plug for the washing machine and the light switch both held very small quantities of what appeared to be blood. No blood was detected on the clothing in the washing machine. This clothing was wet.

'There were spots of what appeared to be blood on the side of the bath, on the bathroom door and on the mat beside the bath. The bath was dry, but there was a quantity of liquid in the bath plug.'

What he didn't record was the fact that one of the police officers had washed their hands in the sink. It dismayed the examiner, but he pressed on.

With the chemist, he moved to the lounge room, where they found the towel on the settee 'stained with what appeared to be blood'. In the bedroom closest to the living room, Huggins couldn't miss the broken blind, with its 'very unstable' catches; in his opinion, it would have dislodged very easily. 'On the bedspread at the foot of the bed, under the window, I saw a quantity of sand and dirt. I formed the opinion that someone had put their foot on the bed possibly when climbing in or out of the window.'

Still in Sue Bartlett's room, he found 'a number of leaf [sic] similar to the leaves that were in an overturned vase in the front bedroom'.

Poignantly, Sergeant Huggins also saw a strand of black thread caught under Sue's body in the hall and running under Suzanne's bedroom door, attached to a reel of thread behind the door.

But it was the walls in the hall that really captured his attention. 'I saw a number of smears and spots of what appeared to be blood on the passage walls on either side of the deceased. On the west wall . . . there was a spray having an upward and northerly direction from fifty centimetres to eighty centimetres from the floor. On the same wall, there was a smear seventy-seven centimetres from the front bedroom door and 100 centimetres from the floor. It had the appearance of a stained hand.'

On the opposite wall, too, Huggins and McBain found 'an area of spots from a point 200 centimetres from the front door for a further 100 centimetres'. In the front bedroom, 'an overturned bottle contain[ing] some plants' was lying at Suzanne Armstrong's left side, 'a pool of what appeared to be blood under head and shoulders'.

As Alf Oldfield, the lead detective at the house that morning, had also observed, there were no signs of an extended struggle in this bedroom. 'The top bedclothes had been folded back from the top left hand corner and a book was open face-down on the corner of the bed,' Huggins noted. 'There were a few spots of what appeared to be blood on the folds of the top sheet. These had been deposited after the sheet had been folded back. There were also a few spots of blood on the chair beside the bed.'

On the bedside table, too, there was what appeared to be blood on the edge of an alarm clock and the switch of the lamp. Here, he could not help but try to explain what this meant, and his theory wasn't pretty. He suspected it was consistent 'with someone having blood on their hand reaching over the bed, smearing blood on the sheet and clock and operating the lamp switch'. He did not elaborate on whether this was likely Suzanne, trying to reach the phone on the bedside table, or her attacker, perhaps trying to switch off the light. Henry Huggins noted that the lamp was off and Suzanne's curtains drawn.

He handed to Moira McBain eight items to enter into evidence: the two blood-stained towels, as well as 'fibres from [the] high chair', the bottom sheet from Susan Bartlett's room, the top and bottom sheets from Suzanne Armstrong's room, Suzanne's clock radio and the panties from beside the bed. The next day, he would enter another item: a face washer, found when Huggins 'examined all the manholes and road drains within two street blocks of No. 147

Easey Street, Collingwood. During this examination, I collected two items – [a] shawl and [a] face washer'.

The final list of exhibits from the house was much more extensive, including what McBain collected herself: 'scrapings' from the side of the bath and the bathroom door, the bath plug and the liquid around it, brown particles from the bath mat, carpet samples from the front bedroom, and the 'scraping' from the passage wall – plus the more personal items that her colleague Sergeant Donohue gathered. It's a confronting collection: one nightie with red and white spots; tubes of blood taken from both women; jars containing samples of their hair, nails and muscle tissue; one green dress; and two tubes containing swabs, one labelled *b, 124 Bartlett, 13/2/77, Vag. smear*, and another labelled *b, 125 13/1/77 Armstrong, Vag.smear.*

A few days after assembling these items for examination, McBain was also given a knife in a sheath to inspect. An eagle-eyed uniformed officer stationed at Collingwood, but not attached to the Easey Street case, had found the 'bloodied knife' in the boot of a car when he was out on patrol conducting vehicle searches, looking for drugs. Constable Ron Iddles had stopped a man in a car and turned up the weapon, promptly delivering it to Homicide, saying, 'The guy claimed he'd found it at Victoria Park railway station, which was a short distance from Easey Street.'

After inspecting all this evidence, McBain determined that Suzanne Armstrong's blood was type A, Susan Bartlett's type O – in other words, both common types. The blood on the towel, carpet and nightdress was A; so too the blood in the bath, in the liquid from the bath plug, on the lamp, the clock radio, both sheets, the knife and a cardigan found in a basket that was a late addition to this evidentiary collection. The three samples taken from the passage wall were type O, as was the blood found on the green dress.

More chillingly, 'spermatozoa were found on both swabs' taken from Suzanne Armstrong, and seminal stains were found on all three sheets in her bedroom, as well as on the carpet and face washer.

There were thirty-six slits in the red-and-white nightie, mainly in the front chest area and on both sides of the left sleeve; twenty-three slits were found in the green dress.

All this forensic information was critical in terms of helping detectives to determine what happened in the house at the time the two women were killed. It gave them a great deal of evidence to work with, which proved invaluable as their investigation continued for months, and then years, and eventually decades, and forensic techniques improved in ways they could not have imagined on that sweaty January day in 1977.

Yet, looking back, the original forensic examiner at 147 Easey Street is not convinced that the evidence was thoroughly examined at the time. Those who examined it didn't pick up what it was telling them – at least not enough to accurately reconstruct what occurred that night.

Henry Huggins, now eighty-eight, remembers the double homicide in Collingwood well. As precise and proper now as in his professional years, he bemoans the unwitting contamination of the crime scene by detectives who were in the house well before he and his forensic team arrived. He is critical, too, of his own official statement, insisting it was not precise enough and would not 'make the grade' in a homicide investigation forty years later.

And he remains unsure exactly how Suzanne was attacked in the front of the house without Sue being aware of what was going on. At least he can speculate unofficially now: perhaps she was out when the murderer entered the house, and came home through the side gate? Or was she out the back when he arrived at the front of the property, doing the washing, pottering around the kitchen?

Rereading his and his colleagues' official statements, he is convinced that it is Suzanne's blood on the sheet in her bedroom, and that she could have been reaching for the telephone on the other side of her bed. He remembers the phone clearly. But it's not visible in the police photographer's shots taken in the room.

It took two days and three nights for Suzanne Armstrong and Sue Bartlett to be found in their inner-city cottage, but their autopsies were underway within hours, at the old Coroner's Court in South Melbourne, in a room behind the court itself.

James McNamara was the senior government pathologist on duty, and for the next four days, the doctor, known to his colleagues as 'Mack the Knife', conducted post-mortem examinations on both bodies. His report, in tandem with Henry Huggins' forensic exhibits, brought to life the girls' final minutes.

Suzanne Armstrong, '167 centimetres in height and weighing 60 kilograms', had been stabbed twenty-seven times. McNamara's external examination revealed seven wounds to her chest, eleven to her left arm, two to the right nipple and a single wound below her left nipple. There was also an 'abrasion' on her left eye and a stab wound to her cheek.

The pathologist's internal exam revealed the attacker's knife had penetrated her heart three times, her left lung seven times and her right lung once; 'the third rib on the left-hand side was cut, with partial severance of the fourth and fifth ribs'. There were also two wounds to her liver, and an 'abraded area' above the vulva.

Susan Bartlett, '170 centimetres in height and weighing 89 kilograms', sustained fifty-five stab wounds, although some seemed to occur in clusters the pathologist couldn't distinguish clearly enough to count as separate wounds: 'A stab wound in the right shoulder region and in the left shoulder region, more stab wounds, with stab wounds present around the left nipple and above the left nipple into the midline of the chest', the report noted.

As Sue struggled with the killer in the hallway of the house, she sustained 'extensive abrasions' to the upper portion of her chest, some eighteen wounds to her arms and seven to her neck. The autopsy recorded a two-and-a-half-centimetre stab wound in the stomach, and two more wounds of similar size to her liver. It was obvious, too, that she was stabbed as she lay face down on the floor, given the number of wounds to her buttocks and thighs.

After listing the ancillary investigations – including a 'routine histopathology, blood for alcohol to Medic-legal laboratory, blood for grouping ... vaginal smears to Forensic Science' – Dr McNamara recorded the official cause of death for both women: 'multiple stab wounds'.

He did not isolate which had been the fatal wounds for either woman. To this day, it remains unclear.

CHAPTER 6

THE FAMILIES

As news of the murders reverberated through Melbourne, and then around Australia, the families of the victims were forced to cope with an all-too-public release of information about the double homicide.

Crime reporters who attended the scene in Easey Street were informed about what had happened inside and quickly published as many details as they could confirm. This meant that both families heard the news second-hand, through the media. Suzanne Armstrong's mother, Eileen, found out as she and her partner, Bruce Currie, were driving back from a holiday in Canberra. They saw the headlines on the front page of a newspaper when they stopped at a service station along the highway, and recognised the women's house from the photographs.

Sue Bartlett's brother, Martin, got a call from his girlfriend, after she heard on the radio about two bodies being found in Collingwood. He immediately rang his sister's home. 'It was on the [Thursday] morning, about 10.30, 10.45 am,' he says. 'I rang the home line and a male answered. I said, "Who's that?"

'He said, "Who are you?"

'I said, "I'm Martin Bartlett, Susan's brother."

'And he said, "Can you come down here?"

'"What for?"

'"We'd just like to talk to you."'

When Martin arrived at Easey Street, he moved through a gathering gauntlet of journalists to speak with this detective in the street. The police wouldn't let him into the house. That didn't upset him. Once he knew what had happened, he had no intention of going in.

But he did want to be the one to tell his mother, Elaine, before she heard it from anyone else. She was staying with a family friend in Benalla, having 'a bit of a break'. After ringing the friend she was with to let him know what had happened, and that he was on his way, Martin made the three-hour drive up the highway to break the shocking news in person.

With sixteen-month-old Gregory safely in care, police managed to contact Suzanne's father, Bill Armstrong, and he told the rest of the family. This must have been gut-wrenching, and it was made even more difficult by the fact that one of his daughters was far from Melbourne, in the outback.

Gayle Armstrong was 1000 kilometres away from home that week in January 1977, working as a cook in a shearing shed in a tiny town called Tilpa, in far west New South Wales. Far, *far* west New South Wales to be exact – further north than Broken Hill and along the Darling River.

Tilpa boasts a population of forty-four, one pub and a cemetery that, according to the Australian Cemeteries Index, 'contains no graves ... the only cemetery in Australia, if not the world, to have no one buried in it'. It is still not easy to reach quickly; it must have been an arduous trek four decades ago.

Yet Suzanne had planned to visit the far-away town, loving the idea of just getting away for a bit. She had been hoping to join her sister – willing to take on the role of 'cook's assistant'. 'I was cooking for shearers at the time, that's what I did,' Gayle explains. 'There were probably six shearers and six other workers to feed, so a dozen all up. I was cooking on a wooden stove in 100-degree heat.' No wonder she was looking forward to having Suzanne by her side. 'She was just going to go up there with me to help me. Not that I really needed it. It was just a break; it was going to be a break for her,' Gayle says.

Suzanne had tried to find someone to mind young Greg for a week or two, so she could make the trip. But neither of her parents, the most likely candidates, could help, and there were no friends she felt she could call on. So Suzanne and her son stayed at home, and she must have felt disappointed, maybe even a bit peeved, about not being able to go. She could not have foreseen how dire this change of plans would prove – a sliding-doors moment with nightmarish consequences.

When Gayle heard the news of her sister's death, she was on her own. 'Well, here I am in the shed, 30 kilometres away from the nearest neighbour,' she recalls, haltingly. 'The police found out where I was, and rang him [the neighbour] and sent a messenger over to me. The contractor took me back to the house and I've got the news … on the phone. From Dad. So then we had to go back to the shed and get my things and then go 200 kilometres or something to get to Broken Hill, bloody hell … to fly home.'

It took two days to make it back to Melbourne, and Bill Armstrong was waiting for her at the airport. Having just identified his oldest daughter's mutilated body, it must have been the greatest relief for him to see Gayle walk off that plane. She went to stay with her mother, and a day or so later decided to visit her boyfriend, Henry Woodard.

The farmhand from Seymour was staying at his sister's place in Northcote, along with his brother, Barry. Barry and Suzanne had been on three dates before her death, and he was the author of the note on the kitchen table at 147 Easey Street.

From the moment Gayle arrived, she says the atmosphere in the house was strange. Tense. Strained. The place seemed unusually dark, she remembers, as she walked down the hall, passing a room closed off behind curtains. Barry Woodard was apparently in that room, too upset to come out to see her.

The visit didn't last long. Suzanne's stoic, independent sister's world was spinning, as the brothers' must have been too, the collective grief overwhelming. 'There was no conversation. I don't even know if I had a cup of tea. And we sat and said whatever we had to say, and so it was time to go, and Henry came out to the car and said goodbye to me and [then] … nothing. It was just eerie. It's always stuck in my head as eerie … the eeriest visit that I've ever had in a house.' Considering the vortex of anguish the week had brought, this wasn't surprising.

Looking back now, it seems odd to Gayle that she and Henry had thought it a good idea to bring Barry and Suzanne together. Barry, in turn, was not fond of her. 'Gayle's a wild one,' he said, years after this awkward visit. 'She was going with my brother at the time, but they broke up after the bodies were discovered. Everything changed then.'

Things certainly did change. As the long, grim week wore on, the ordeal seemed to worsen for the Armstrong family. They waited to hear from the police, expecting to be told more about what, precisely, had happened to Suzanne and her friend Sue, and about police leads on the person who did it. But over the next few days, they heard nothing at all from the detectives working on the case. Eventually, unable to stand not knowing what was happening with the investigation, they rang the police and asked if they could come in to see them. 'It was terrible,' says Gayle. '*We* had to go down to the police station, I remember; we had to go down to Russell Street. We had to get in the car and go to them.'

That wasn't the only upsetting event they had to confront. Suzanne's and Susan's funerals had to be organised – a task almost too much for both families. Martin Bartlett was the only one able to step into the role of planner. Back in Melbourne again, having helped his mother through the initial distress of learning of her daughter's death, the 25-year-old kept it simple. 'I had to,' he says now. He organised one service for the two friends.

The 'Armstrong/Bartlett funeral' was a heart-rending ceremony in the Blair Chapel at Springvale Crematorium. With only ten chairs available for the family to share, some fifty people stood to farewell the two women, including senior reporter Mike Roberts from *The Age*:

> 'I would like there to be no minimising of the brutality and wrongfulness. Evil is a reality,' the Rev. Geoff Crouch, Susan

Bartlett's uncle, told the gathering.

The crowded little chapel was hot, and here and there a man slipped his jacket off. 'How much are we responsible for the kind of society that we have?' asked Rev. Alan Lock, a friend of the Armstrongs'. 'Those of us here find it hard to understand the pressures of those inner suburbs. Yet they chose to live in that area to express something of their personalities and their involvement and understanding of others.'

And soon it was over, a 25-minute service nine days after a brutal murder.

But to Martin, the ritual seemed anti-climactic. 'Obviously, at that stage there was an ongoing inquiry, no result and no real leads. Never found a murder weapon,' he says.

One of the things that bothered him about the investigation was the uncertainty around *when* his sister and her friend were attacked. If he left their house between 9.00 and 9.30 pm on that Monday night, 10 January, and their bodies were found at 9.30 am on Thursday morning, 13 January, had they died not long after he left, or had it been on one of the two subsequent evenings? He hounded the detectives about this at the time. 'I was always asking about the timeline. [But] because it [took] so long to actually do the autopsy, the time of death was difficult to determine.'

Harder again was the impact that his sister's death had on their mother. 'For her to understand why someone would do it, and to do it to her daughter ... really, just over the years her blood pressure went through the roof,' Martin says. 'She died at sixty-one. It just killed her in the end. It was just such a stressful thing that she never, ever came to grips with why someone would do it. Even if they had found somebody, she would not have comprehended why that person could have done what they did.'

A devastated Bill Armstrong did not live long after his daughter's murder either, succumbing to severe burns after becoming trapped fighting a bushfire around Bairnsdale in January 1978. Less than a year after they had lost Suzanne, the Armstrong family was reduced in number again.

CHAPTER 7

THE 'VISITORS'

ONE OF THE sixty people attending Blair Chapel for the funeral of Suzanne Armstrong and Susan Bartlett was the man who had recently started seeing Suzanne. He was also now a significant 'person of interest' to investigators. He had to be. He entered 147 Easey Street between the time his new girlfriend and Sue were last seen alive and when their bodies were discovered.

Worried that he had not been able to reach Suzanne by phone, Barry Woodard and his brother visited the house two nights after the women were killed, at approximately 8.30 pm. They called out to her, then left a note on the table under an ashtray in the kitchen.

The brothers maintained that they didn't go further than the kitchen and so did not see the bodies lying at the other end of the small cottage. Nor did they hear Greg in his cot, two rooms away, up the hall. They have never deviated from this explanation of their incongruous nocturnal visit.

Barry, a 31-year-old shearer from Euroa, had known Suzanne longer than the two weeks they had been going out, and there was already a family connection, due to 24-year-old Henry's relationship with her sister, Gayle. From the time he had gone on a blind date with Suzanne, arranged by Gayle and Henry, they had a good rapport, and he felt it was odd that Suzanne had not returned his calls after they'd had dinner at his sister's house in Northcote on Sunday night, 9 January. He last saw her around midnight, after dropping her home.

'She had been with me at my sister's place in Northcote for tea,' he recounted. 'I took her and her son Gregory home to Easey Street later that night. Sue Bartlett was there, and also a man friend of hers. He drives a white Mercedes.'

He had a cup of coffee with them and left, getting back to his sister's place about fifteen minutes later. 'The next morning I was expecting a phone call from a cocky [a sheep farmer] because I was supposed to go shearing. Actually, Suzanne asked me to stay at her place on the Sunday night, but because I was expecting this phone call and I would have had to get up early, I did not stay.'

Not even the formal language used in these old transcripts of police interviews and in the coroner's statement can dispel the sad inevitability of the chain of events.

'Anyhow, the next morning I did not get the phone call. I got out of bed about 9.30, 10.00 am and stopped around the house. Later on in the afternoon, I tried to ring Suzanne to tell her I did not have to go to work.'

He kept calling throughout the afternoon.

'She was supposed to come to our place for tea on Tuesday, and I wanted to talk to her about that. There was no answer when I rang.' He told police that he stayed home until about 5.30 pm, when he and his brother, Henry, went to the Albion Charles Hotel in St Georges Road for a drink.

At about 7.00 pm, they arrived back at his sister's place. 'I got some bottles and we ... sat around home drinking ... for a while and had tea at half-past eight. After tea, we sat down and watched TV. I seem to remember trying to ring Suzanne again at about ten o'clock, but there was no answer. So I think I went to bed a bit after that. I slept in the front room on my own. I stayed in bed all night and got up at about eight o'clock on Tuesday.'

He added that he had parked his car out the front of the house in Northcote when he and his brother got back from the pub, 'but later moved it to a side street'.

Police didn't ask him why he did that, nor did they press his sister on the issue when she gave them her statement. But she certainly vouched for her brother's whereabouts that night.

'Barry has been with me for a few years now. He is a shearer by occupation and he travels around working, but usually comes home at weekends. My brother Henry also stays at my place from time to time,' she told detectives. 'Barry used to sleep in the shop part of our place. It used to be a shop at one time.'

That weekend, their sister Cheryl and her four children were also staying with Margaret, her husband, Max, and their four children – so 'we were a little bit crowded, with all the children and adults sleeping everywhere'. Suzanne Armstrong and her toddler had been there too, on the Sunday. But police were more interested in what occurred the next night at Margaret's busy family home. Max, Barry and Cheryl went to the hotel for a couple of hours, she told them, and returned at about 7.00 pm. They brought back about a dozen or more bottles of beer and the group sat around talking and drinking.

'Cheryl wanted to go back to Yea, and Barry was going to drive her back on the Tuesday, but he was going to leave early as he wanted to be back because Sue [Suzanne] was coming for tea.'

She said her brother went to bed on Monday night 'possibly around midnight, because we did not have tea until about 10.30 pm. Cheryl stayed up talking to me; my husband had gone to bed and my brother Henry and his girlfriend had gone to bed in the lounge room.'

Margaret recalled that she and her sister stayed up chatting until 'about 2.00 am, because I had to feed my baby around that time and I did not want to go to bed for half an hour and then get up to feed him'.

She could not be sure 'who slept where' in the crowded house that night but suggested her sister would have 'either slept in my daughter's bed, or in the bed in the shop next to Barry's bed'. There were two single beds in that room. 'If Cheryl slept in my daughter's bed, then two of her children would have slept in the shop in one bed, and another one in the bed with Barry, and some of the other children in the fold-up bed and on the mattress.'

Initially, she couldn't recall if she or her sister went into the shop before retiring for the night, or whether the next time she saw Barry was when she took him a cup of coffee early on Tuesday morning. 'I would have been up about 6.00 or 6.30 am to feed my baby, as he was on four-hourly feeds at that time. My usual practice was to feed the baby and make coffee and take a cup up to Barry, as he would always be awake. I cannot remember doing this on the Tuesday, but imagine that I would have.'

She would later tell the coroner that she was certain she did, in fact, take her brother a cup of coffee that morning. She was also adamant that before he drove Cheryl and her children home to Yea, Barry asked her to call Suzanne to see what time she wanted to be picked up for tea. 'I rang Sue's number at about 2.00 pm, but got no answer.'

On his return to Melbourne that afternoon, he continued to call the Easey Street house, and the women's phone continued to ring out. But it wasn't until late on Wednesday afternoon that Barry Woodard became seriously concerned. After calling several times that afternoon, he and his brother decided to drive to Collingwood that evening, to see what was going on.

They got to Easey Street between 8.30 and 8.45 pm, having driven over in Barry's white HD Holden sedan. 'I saw a note on the front door, but I did not read it,' he told police. 'We went around to the back of the house, and the side gate and back door were open and the kitchen light was on. I mean, they were about half open. I knocked on the back door and yelled out for Suzanne, but there was no answer. Henry put an envelope with my name on it and phone number on the kitchen table near the telephone.'

He tried to explain why he didn't go any further into the house. 'I do not like going into other people's houses when no one is there. I did not know Suzanne well enough to just go into her house.'

Barry claimed he and his brother were only in the kitchen for about five minutes before driving back to his sister's place in Northcote. 'I did not notice anything unusual at Suzanne's address,' he insisted to police. 'I got the opinion that she was not far away, because the door and the gate were open and the kitchen light was on.'

Tragically, of course, he was right.

'When I got home, I rang Susan's number again. But again there was no answer. The next time I rang was this morning, when I spoke to a Homicide Squad detective who told me what had happened.'

That detective told him to stay where he was. They would be around to speak with him shortly. And they were, taking him back to the Russell Street police headquarters for lengthy questioning later that morning.

His brother, Henry, also recalled walking up to the front door and seeing a note stuck on it. 'But I could not understand it. We then knocked on the door, but there was no answer, so we went around the back door and saw the kitchen light was on and the back gate and back door were *wide* open,' the farmhand said. 'We yelled out two or three times for Suzanne, but there was no answer. We both walked into the kitchen and yelled out again, but there was no answer. Then Barry said to leave a note, so I put it on the kitchen table with [his] telephone number on it. I did not see or hear anything unusual when I was at the house.'

Having come all the way to find Suzanne, Henry was keen to step into the hallway and see if she was at home, perhaps in one of the front rooms. But his older brother didn't want him to go past the kitchen. 'I wanted to walk through the house, but Barry said not to. I saw the corridor door was open also but I did not look up there.'

The brothers retraced their steps as they left the house, walking out the back door, through the gate and up the lane to the street, before driving home to their sister's.

Once there, Henry said his brother tried to ring Suzanne three or four more times before going to bed. Really worried now,

Henry tried again too, at about 2.00 am on the next morning. Again, no answer.

Eight hours later, the Woodard brothers would know why.

Of course, the brothers' visit to the house two nights after the murders still raises questions. Have they remembered any new information from that night? Did they ever wonder if they saw something significant they didn't understand at the time?

But forty years on, Barry does not want to answer questions. In many ways, who can blame him? Dogged by the double homicide for two decades before finally being cleared of any involvement in the crime by two DNA tests, no doubt he feels he's been through enough public scrutiny. So when I rang him in mid-November 2017, he was polite but firm. 'I don't want nothing to do with it,' he said. As I tried to outline the research I was conducting for this book, he continued, 'Let me stop you right there. I'm sorry, but I don't want to meet you.' A woman in the background was talking too, and seemed to be asking who he was speaking to. 'No, no, I don't want anything to do with it. No, no. Thank you for calling, but I don't want to meet you or talk to you. Goodbye.'

Back in 1977, police soon came to realise something quite extraordinary: the Woodards were not the only visitors to 147 Easey Street after the murders had occurred. Two other men had visited the house on Tuesday night, one even climbing through Sue Bartlett's window and walking into the hallway while his friend waited outside in the lane. It was his footprint that the team of detectives had noticed during the first walk-through of the murder scene.

The tobacco salesman, who has never been publicly named, was a relatively new acquaintance of Sue's and had also been calling the house, trying to reach her. But the phone rang out so many times, he thought he must have had the wrong number. He decided to go and see her.

With his male friend as backup, he drove to Collingwood and walked along the lane until he reached her bedroom window. With a bit of a leg-up from his mate, he climbed in, stepping on her bed in the process, walked through the unlit room and turned right at the passageway, where he moved towards the telephone in the lounge room. After checking the number on the dial and realising he had been calling the right one all along, he claimed he retraced his steps back up the hall and into Sue's room and out the window, where his friend was still waiting in the laneway.

He was adamant that he did not see her body, or hear Greg crying in the cot in the room next to Sue's; in fact, he didn't know anything was wrong until he saw a copy of *The Herald* newspaper late on Thursday 13 January.

'An American friend of mine walked into my room ... He had a copy of *The Herald* and said, "Hey, isn't this your new girlfriend?" There was a story about the murders on the front page,' he would recount to journalist Tom Prior some twenty years later. 'I said "wacky do, wacky do" and went to see the police.'

But not before heeding the advice of yet another friend, who insisted he take a lawyer with him. 'And it is probably just as well that I did. The police gave me an extremely hard time, particularly when I admitted I had returned to Easey Street on the Tuesday night to check the telephone number.

'I had been calling what turned out to be the right number without getting an answer all day. I had no idea what was going on. When I reached Easey Street, the front of the house was in darkness, but the light was on in the kitchen.

'I had been drinking, and probably had a few too many. I stepped in the middle of the bed in Sue's room and knocked down the blind . . . they "grilled" me, like they do in the movies. I just couldn't believe it. I could have been blamed for the murders. Sometimes I think I nearly was.

'I was upset and used to think about the murders a lot. I still do occasionally; it was very traumatic. What would have happened if I had wandered into the murderer? Would I have tackled him, or would I have run?'

These are difficult, personally confronting questions. To be fair, if the only light on in the house was the one in the kitchen, the corridor would have been dark. But if that was so, how did he see the number on the telephone? Was the kitchen light bright enough to illuminate it? He passed *so* close to Greg and the women's bodies as he stumbled his way in and out of their home that it's hard to comprehend that he didn't sense something was wrong: 'I did not see a thing, let alone the body of Susan Bartlett in the passage. I did not look,' he told police. Had he looked, of course, the police would have been called sooner, and the investigation would have begun much earlier. By the time the women's bodies were found on Thursday 13 January, the forty-eight-hour window – which investigators often say is the most crucial in solving a case – had already closed.

But this visitor to Easey Street must not have been a serious suspect in the case, despite the 'grilling' he remembers police gave him at the time. Perhaps impressed that he had come to see them so quickly, they allowed him to leave the country in March that year. This meant that one of the three men who admitted being inside the house where two women lay dead for two days and three nights in January was overseas, travelling, when the coroner's inquest was held in July.

Decades later, DNA testing would decisively clear him, along with the Woodard brothers, of any involvement with the murders. But the families were left to speculate: might the police investigation have taken a more positive course had one of these men seen something and raised the alarm earlier?

CHAPTER 8

THE NEIGHBOURS

As the weeks dragged on, the detectives assigned to the double homicide came under mounting pressure. Not only did they need to find the women's killer, but they also had to calm a city on edge.

Usually staid Melbourne was gripped by a sense of alarm. A murderer was at large, a man who could brutally overpower two women in their own home. And no one seemed to know who he was. The ferocity of the killings made even the most confident within the community, plus those who were already uneasy about the rising drug use and crime rates of the time, double-check their doors and windows as they retired for the night.

From the earliest news reports, there seemed to be consensus among journalists that one or both of the women had either known their attacker and let him into the house, or that he had somehow got under their guard – let himself in through an open door, and then taken their lives in the most violent way. Either scenario was, of course, terrifying – especially to other young women living in inner-city Melbourne.

As criminologist and former Easey Street resident Dean Wilson summarises nearly two generations later, it was a tale of gothic proportion. 'There [was] a kind of moral undertone to the story, the sense that if you were a young, independent woman, you'd be murdered. It was a rented house in the 1970s with a lot of young people in and out of it,' he says. 'For some Melbournians, conservative Melbournians, it was a tale ripped from the side of Melbourne [author] Helen Garner wrote about. The "other side". What's interesting about it was there was this sense that there's a danger about and all young women should lock themselves away ... It had *Monkey Grip* written all over it.'

In fact, Helen Garner followed the media reports of the investigation closely. 'I remember it vividly. It happened in the seventies and that was smack in the middle of the period of the great flourishing of collective or communal households in Melbourne,' she recalled, nearly thirty years later, in 2005. 'That was the period when I lived in that sort of household, and when we read about those murders in the paper it made our blood run cold, because it could have happened to us.

'They were very innocent times in the sense that we didn't lock our doors, the key was in the front door, and people walked in and out of houses in quite a casual way,' she said. 'And we were always going out to pubs and dancing the night away, and sometimes one would come home with a person one had only just met. Those are things that we did in those days. I look back on it with incredulity in a way – the sort of unguardedness of our lives. So we had a very lively interest in the story.'

For many, what made the murders even harder to read about, and impossible to ignore, was the presence of the little boy. Left unharmed, yet alone, in his cot for three nights and two days, with no food and no water, his mother's body just metres away.

The police tried to reassure the inner-city community that their investigation was progressing quickly. They were pretty sure they had a key suspect well and truly in sight. And it wasn't any of the three men who entered Easey Street following the women's deaths.

Following the murders, the detectives had been back a number of times to inspect the house in Easey Street that, for days, had been a shroud, to make sure they had not missed anything. They were now locating family members, friends, neighbours – anyone who might be able to help them fill in the awful hours between 9.30 pm on Monday night and early the following morning, when the examiners believed the girls had died.

Police plundered the women's address books and Suzanne's diary for possible contacts to follow up: if they could track what the two had been doing in the days preceding their deaths, find out who they had been with, they might be able to ascertain if anything out of the ordinary had occurred. Had either Suzanne Armstrong or Sue Bartlett mentioned anyone troubling them recently?

Given the timeframe in which they believed the killings had occurred, they were also hopeful someone in the neighbourhood might be able to help paint a picture. It was summer holidays. Maybe one of the kids who lived in the street had been out on their bike that balmy evening and noticed someone entering the house a bit later than might be expected. Perhaps a local on his or her way home from one of the nearby hotels had passed someone in a hurry, later still.

There were two pubs nearby, both just a few minutes' walk from the women's house. The Leinster Arms was probably the most accessible of the pair, on the corner of Gold and Hotham streets; the Bendigo Hotel was on the busier location of Gold and Johnston. Both would have closed at midnight.

Phillip Perez's parents lived in the street. After coming to Australia from Portugal, they moved from Fitzroy to Collingwood in the mid-1970s, where they started a family. They were part of the influx of migrants in the area during the 1960s and early 1970s; European families – primarily Greek and Italian, but also Spanish and Portuguese – took Collingwood to heart, planting vegetable and flower gardens in their yards, grapevines mingling with old-fashioned rose bushes. They appreciated how close they were to Clifton Hill, Richmond and the city – many walked to work each day. Several of these residents still live in Easey Street today, entertaining grandchildren in the long-established gardens they planted as their children went to school and played outside in the street nearly half a century ago.

In 1977, Phillip was five and a half years older than Suzanne's son, but still young enough to play in his blow-up pool. He recollects running up the lane along the side of Greg's house to get to the backyard. 'It used to be wide open,' he says, leaning forward on his knees as he pictures it. 'I used to … walk straight into the backyard and play with the kid. I was wandering everywhere at that age. Mum said I used to love going into the street.'

The Perez family rented 127 Easey Street for five years, before buying a property immediately behind it in Sackville Street, the first of several they would come to own in the area. A much-loved

Tuscan-style garden that his mother, Josephine, has tended for forty years sits between a couple of small houses there now, one of which she lives in. All up, he estimates the 'family estate' covers about 1900 metres – 'something like that' – a developer's dream that was unimaginable two generations ago.

But Phillip remembers a livelier Collingwood, when there were more people in the streets. 'Kids, the Greeks and everybody all mixed in the street,' he says with a nod. 'Australian, everybody, all mixed in Easey Street. All the kids would go out and play in the streets with their BMXs and dragsters and everybody was talking to each other. Everyone was more open. Yeah, everybody would just go to each other's barbeques.'

There were also rough elements in the neighbourhood, and there was no escaping them, even for a child. 'There was one family, probably a Greek family, they robbed banks and stuff. And I remember once I was about to walk out the front door – I was only ten years old – and heard *bang, bang, bang*. You know, you think, "What's that noise, a car backfiring?" And then you hear police sirens, walk out the front door and there's a VW Kombi at the end of the street with bullet holes in the back and the police all there – and these guys are running up the side of this car and then they're jumping the roofs and up in the lane, and the police are saying, "Stay indoors!" It was stuff like that going on … a bit rough, I reckon.'

Phillip knew all about the gangs roaming Collingwood and its sister suburbs: the Collingwood Boys and the Collingwood Dump Boys, bumping up against the Richmond Boys and the Fitzroy Boys. There were skinheads and sharpies, many of the groups based around the housing commission high-rise apartments. 'If you'd go to the commission flats here in Collingwood, there'd be a gang in there, and then you've got the other housing commission at Clifton Hill, there'd be a gang up there. And then you'd go to Carlton, the same thing. It'd be more Maoris in the Carlton flats, but in Collingwood, it's all mixed. It was Aussies and Turks and Spanish, Greek, you know? Whatever it was, it was all mixed in Collingwood.'

Phillip Perez also remembers the police presence in the area, and the bias often shown towards young men. 'Oh, you'd be walking down the street and they'd pull you up and give you a hard time, ask a million questions. I remember that. We were cheeky anyway, so ...'

Into this mix came a new wave of renters, younger, artistic people such as Suzanne Armstrong and Sue Bartlett, some of them single, some in couples, some working, some students, sharing the little houses often owned by their neighbours.

Josephine Perez remembers the women who moved into 147 Easey Street late in 1976, especially Suzanne, who would often be out walking with her son in his pram. Phillip was on the street the morning police arrived and cordoned off the house, and he ran to tell his mother that something was going on. 'He didn't understand because he was too young,' Josephine says. 'But there were too many people in the street [for it to be nothing]. I decided I'm going there to see.'

She arrived in time to watch two bodies being wheeled out of the narrow front door on gurneys and placed in what she remembers as an ambulance, but was actually the undertaker's van.

Another neighbour, who had moved into Easey Street in 1970, came out of her house too to see the crowd gathered down near

Hoddle Street. She already suspected that all was not quite right that day, having experienced something the night before the women's bodies were discovered that she still can't explain. It was a man's voice saying, 'Somebody kill the two teachers tonight.'

'It was either a dream or someone walking past in the middle of the night,' 85-year-old Christina Fourtouris insists. 'I wake up in the morning, I say to my husband, to my kids – because I had a boy and a girl – "something happened: someone passed, or I'm dreaming, I'm not sure."'

When she eventually went outside later, she saw a street full of residents, and a swarm of police. 'I say, "What happened down there?"'

'Killed the two teachers' came the reply, according to Fourtouris. Although, of course, only Sue was a teacher.

'I said, "What?"'

She waited to tell police about what she believed she had heard as they door-knocked up and down the street over the next few days, searching for information. But they didn't come to her door. She didn't try to contact them, either; she knew her story sounded crazy. She knew they would think she was just a 'crazy Greek woman'.

Mrs Fourtouris would say 'hello, good morning' to her two neighbours as she walked to her job as a machinist in Richmond and Suzanne cycled past with Greg on the back of the bike or Susan headed off to Collingwood High. 'Nice girls, I can tell you. One tall – Susan, I think – and the other one a little bit shorter.' She remembers Greg Armstrong as tall for his age, a toddler who loved to play outside with his dog.

All these years later, she is unwavering that she heard a voice in the street in the pre-dawn hours of 13 January. 'The night [it] happen, somebody say, "Kill the two teachers tonight." That's it. Nothing else.'

And Christina wasn't the only person living in Easey Street who had something to share with police and was never questioned by detectives. Two residents living much closer to the 'murder house' had something even more dramatic to reveal.

CHAPTER 9

THE WITNESSES

GLADYS COVENTRY LIVED at 145 Easey Street with her husband, Thomas William Clyde Coventry. Their cottage overlooked the same little lane as 147 Easey Street.

Born in Tasmania in 1893, Tom had lived in Collingwood with his mother, Mary Elizabeth Coventry, since the 1930s. A long-time local, he saw monumental change in the community in his decades in the little house. The milkman would still have been delivering from his horse-drawn cart up and down the street when Tom and his mother arrived in the suburb, though by 1977 the bluestone 'dunny lane' had not been used for its original purpose for many years.

Nonetheless, it provided a thoroughfare to a narrower alley that ran along the back of his house and the three next to it. This allowed the Coventrys a unique perspective on their immediate community. The couple could look over their hip-high wooden fence bordering the lane and see their neighbours coming and going.

Gladys Coventry could also see quite a lot from her kitchen window, near which she sat most nights – in front of the fireplace for warmth in winter, and on hot summer evenings, to catch any breeze that blew through the little house to make Melbourne's sticky nights bearable. She could see into the kitchen of the house next door if the lights were on.

The elderly woman, believed to be in her early eighties at the time of the murders, cared for her ailing 84-year-old husband, and from all accounts was undaunted by the fact that her hearing had started to fade and other indignities of age were creeping up on her. She was embedded in the community, having moved in with Tom some time after his mother died in 1963; she first appeared on the electoral roll as an Easey Street resident in 1968. So she knew everyone who lived around them, and had watched many of them grow up over the years. And they all knew her, 'the little old lady in 145'. They would see her go shopping, pulling her trolley behind her, never accepting a lift as she walked to the bus stop, heading for Victoria Market, or trundled over to the milk bar, with her slight stoop, as well-dressed as she could manage. Her neighbours knew her routine, as she did theirs.

But Mrs Coventry saw someone on the night of the murders, that Monday night in January 1977 – someone it seems she did not recognise. There's no police statement recording her testimony, let alone an Identikit sketch that could have helped identify a suspect. Gladys Coventry tried to tell detectives what she had seen, yet they never took her full account. But at least a couple recall her unsettling story, and before she died more than a decade after the murders, she told one of her neighbours what she witnessed that night.

In the kitchen at 147 Easey Street, a man was washing his hands at the sink, over and over – and he seemed to be scrubbing at a piece of cloth or clothing, too. Whatever he was doing, he didn't seem to be in a hurry to get it done or to leave the house.

When he eventually walked out the back door and stepped through her neighbours' side gate, into the laneway, she might have pulled back, just a little. For a second, they would have been just metres apart, but he couldn't see her as she sat in her cool, dark kitchen.

Then he was gone.

Late as it was, the long-term Collingwood resident probably didn't think much more about this close encounter, at least not immediately. He must have seemed like just another of the women's friends, someone who knew them well enough to be using their kitchen and leaving by the back door. He appeared at ease walking around the house, not in any hurry. A good two days would probably pass before she thought of that man washing his hands again.

But on Thursday morning she might have heard Ilona Stevens yelling out from the back of the house across the lane. 'Call the police,' Ilona was telling someone in the next house. 'They're dead.'

A little later, too, she would have seen the tall woman with the black hair talking to a young uniformed officer at the side gate of 147, then older men swarming up the lane and into the house next door, and two bodies being taken out the front door on gurneys. Was it the two young women she had seen, only recently, the little boy in tow? She would have quickly surmised that it had to be. And suddenly it must have been apparent how important what she had seen nights earlier could prove to be.

She tried to talk to the police. But the nattily dressed detectives from Homicide didn't really listen, she felt; not properly. They didn't ignore her, exactly, but they didn't really give her the time of day, and she didn't like the tone they took. So she simply stopped talking to them.

Appreciating that they had somehow offended possibly their only witness, the Homicide team came up with a strategy to prise more information from her, enlisting a police doctor to visit the house and discuss the murders. But Gladys Coventry realised what he was up to and sent him packing.

No one pressed her for more detail after that. Nor did they insist she see their sketch artist to provide details for a portrait of the suspect.

More than forty years later, this astonishing oversight still troubles the few who knew about it at the time. They believe it's where the investigation started to go wrong. It's certainly the first thing former detective Brian 'The Skull' Murphy recalls about the case. 'They buggered it up,' he says, matter-of-factly. 'Right from the start.'

Once one of Victoria's most controversial senior officers, Murphy, now retired, has been the subject of two books examining his tumultuous career and the high-profile cases he investigated. No doubt there are more stories to tell for the detective who, as *Age* reporter John Silvester noted in a 2017 profile of him, 'was charged (and acquitted) of homicide, caused a Royal Commission, was falsely accused of an underworld murder and was the subject of several corruption inquiries that always failed to implicate Murphy in anything illegal'.

This 'copper' heard things while on the job. He heard that Gladys Coventry told the detectives that she had seen a man washing his hands in the kitchen of the women's house, but that the octogenarian clammed up because she didn't like the way the young men from Homicide were talking to her. 'It was alleged the coppers upset her,' the retired detective says.

He believes his colleagues would probably have been impatient, too full of themselves, in their suits and ties, with their murders to solve, to give Mrs Coventry the time she deserved to tell them her story. 'Maybe they were smartarses ... Homicide were a pack of smartarses in those days. Arrogant bastards, they were.' He suggests that the doctor called on to visit the elderly neighbour might have been John Birrell, Victoria's police surgeon. 'This was a woman with a fair bit of age on her, they went and got a doctor to see if she'd enlighten him about it. She sprung him!' Brian Murphy laughs, with a gruff delight.

If he's right, and Dr Birrell was called to Collingwood, it meant that one of the country's most lauded medical officers was assisting in the case, highlighting not only the prominence of the double murders but also the significance police placed on trying to get Gladys Coventry's eyewitness account.

Renowned around the world for his campaigning against drink driving, John Birrell is thought to have helped save around 30,000 lives through his support of harsher drink-driving laws, blood-alcohol testing and compulsory seatbelts. But if it was Birrell who was sent in to see Gladys Coventry, none of this was enough to convince her to talk to him or his colleagues. According to Murphy, he wasn't straightforward with her, which probably didn't help. 'I think he told her he'd come for a welfare check, something like that,' Murphy says. 'But they chose the wrong bloke to send in to talk to her. He was a very properly spoken man, very plummy, and she wouldn't have liked that – not to mention he was about six-foot-thirteen, with a bald head and built like a German tank. It was a bad choice – she picked him straight away. She said, "You're a friggin' copper!"'

Murphy recalls that police soon became aware they had missed the chance to get a description of a man who had been in the house the night the two women were killed. 'They took it seriously, but when she knocked the cops back, that was it. When it went pear-shaped, they wrote it off.'

Why? There were other murders to solve, other cases to work. These soon took precedence. But Murphy remains aghast at this opportunity lost. 'I don't believe she knew him [the man she saw], but she could have described him – and I think that would have gone a long way to solving the matter.'

In 1987, Hugh Parry-Jones struck up a friendship with Gladys Coventry. Moving in a few doors up, the street's newest resident started using the lane that ran along the side of her house. He was clearing out his backyard and would strike up conversation with his older neighbour whenever he saw her.

Hugh was fascinated by his rather eccentric neighbour, who was in her nineties by the time he met her – 'this classic, really old-school' woman whose husband had died years before. Tom Coventry might have left her with a name that was almost sacred at the Collingwood Football Club – the great Gordon Coventry being the first AFL player to kick one hundred goals in a season – but their little rented house was tumbling down around her, the ramshackle side fence missing more than a few palings.

Mrs Coventry's kitchen, the room she seemed to spend most time in, was little more than 'a really poor-quality lean-to on the back of the house – the place was just a shambles, totally falling down; dark, gloomy, damp. The kitchen was an earth floor, and she would just sit there in front of the fireplace, you know, throughout winter, because she didn't have any heating,' Hugh says.

By the time he got to know her, she was 'really little and hunched', with 'an English accent, or a very refined Australian one – she was a lady, a very polite lady'. Gladys Coventry was quite deaf by this stage and had gone bald years before. 'She had this series of wigs that would sit oddly on her, and sometimes when she went out to do the shopping, she wouldn't realise ... and she had all her makeup in the wrong place. And she dressed like a dowager from some sort of Agatha Christie novel.'

He believes she only had one regular visitor, an older man who would come and join her in the kitchen, where they would talk for hours.

Hugh 'sort of took a shine' to Mrs Coventry. 'I was making a lot more use of the laneway, coming and going, and I would often say to her, "Look, is there something I can do for you? Can I help you, can I fix that up?" She was very nice to me, too.'

A history teacher, Hugh knew the fate of the two women who had lived and died so close by, and eventually he asked his neighbour if she remembered anything of that time. 'One day I said to her, "Given the paucity of the fence palings and privacy, and the fact that you're always up here, what do you know about the murders?" And she goes, "Oh, yes, oh, I've never forgotten that night. I was sitting here!" And you know, she probably was, at three o'clock in the morning, or whenever it happened. Just sitting there and she saw the light come on ... I dare say she might have even had her window open.'

She went on to tell him what she saw. But this time, the account had one more important detail. She said the man she saw leave the women's house that night was carrying a knife. 'And she said, "I saw this bloke and he had a knife, and I told the police and they didn't take it any further. The police said they'd come back to talk to me, but they never did. They didn't believe me, they didn't take me seriously." She was cranky, she really was. And you can imagine – to a young copper, she'd be older than his grandmother. They probably thought she was a confabulist who was really asleep. It was the times, too; we didn't have the same respect for the elderly we have now.'

Had she mentioned this extraordinary fact about the knife to police ten years before? Or was it an embellishment of time, the kind people often make when remembering even the most important things? Certainly, Gladys Coventry's main point was the same: she had seen a man at 147 Easey Street on the night or in the early morning after the girls were killed.

Hugh was fascinated by what his neighbour told him. 'I said, "Well, what did he look like?"' More than a decade later, she wasn't keen to go back over it. '"Ah, no, I can't remember," she said. "But I gave them a description."'

Kind man that he is, Hugh didn't hassle his elderly neighbour any further, yet remains incredulous that the police didn't press her for as much information as she could provide in the days after the brutal murders were uncovered. 'She would be the most likely person to have witnessed anything, if there was anything ... she was so well-placed to be someone who would have some sort of evidence. But the cops just totally went down the path of all these mystery guys.'

He wanted to believe what Mrs Coventry told him, even knowing that the first set of detectives hadn't set much store in recording her testimony. 'She was very old and it's like, you know, some of the things [she says] don't really gel with reality, so you think, well, maybe that's just another fantasy or something.'

But a little later, when this Easey Street resident walks through his backyard and into the narrow alley running into the wider bluestone lane next to what was once Gladys Coventry's home, he points to where her kitchen would have been. And from this vantage point, it *does* gel with reality. If Mrs Coventry was sitting up that night, gazing out her kitchen window, as she usually did, she would have been staring right at the women's house, their kitchen adjacent with hers.

'I so much wanted to believe her, because like I say, it's location, location, location, and seriously, you can't do much better than that,' Hugh says. 'I mean, if I'd had the opportunity to talk to someone that owned the lodging house that Jack the Ripper had done his last murder in, as recently as ten years later, I think I would have talked to them as much as I could too, you know?'

When Gladys Coventry learnt what had happened to her two young neighbours, and that summer waned without their attacker being apprehended, was she scared? With only her ageing husband to protect her, did she worry that the man she had seen the night the 'two Sues' died might return to hurt them?

Hugh has a theory about who the man could have been. Easey Street was originally a block longer, but had been shortened when Hoddle Street was widened to feed into the new freeway, which finally opened in late 1977. Major construction was still underway in the area that January; even closer was the work being done to finish building the Collingwood Community Health Centre in Sackville Street that backed up to the yards of 149 and 147. Could a worker on one of these sites have been the murderer? Hugh believes this is a strong possibility. 'What is built directly behind the "murder house" was under construction at the time of the murder. So I've always held the theory that there are tradies working on the site – you know, doing roofing, who knows what. They're looking over into this backyard that's got two very attractive young women. It's a heatwave. It's January. So they're at home in the backyard, perhaps drawing attention. In those days, itinerant tradies, day workers, you come and go. How are the cops ever going to track them?

'I still think that site's a really good avenue [for inquiry], because it's such a randomly horrible crime. I don't think it was someone they knew who had a grievance. I don't think they'd leave the baby.'

Standing in the lane that backs up to the brick wall of the health centre now called CoHealth, thinking back to that summer of '77, the history teacher's theory about the builders and tradesmen does not seem far-fetched. 'There may well have even been tradies making their way up and down [this laneway] all day. Again, that just widens the field of people who could see a couple of young attractive women on holidays in a hot summer.'

The bluestone lane has been gated and locked for years now. Initially, this was to keep out the junkies who started using it to shoot up, dropping their needles when they left. Hugh Parry-Jones still wonders if the killer dropped his knife there too, somewhere in the rubbish and weeds, as he came out the side gate. 'He might have flung a murder weapon over into my laneway,' he muses. Investigators never found anything at the time.

Did Hugh ever find a knife, as he cleared the narrow alley that led to his yard? 'No. No. Didn't stop me looking, though.'

The neighbour who lives between Gladys Coventry's old house and Hugh has been there for nearly sixty years. Edie Haines worked all her life at a sock factory in Lygon Street, and she 'couldn't complain about living in Easey Street'. She remembers the Coventrys next door well, even though Mrs Coventry didn't often interact with those around her. 'She was a funny lady, elderly even then,' Mrs Haines says. 'She wouldn't speak to you. I used to say "hello, how are you?" and she'd just look away, she'd never reply.'

The memory makes her chuckle now. But that's not to say she doubts the veracity of what Gladys Coventry tried to tell the police in 1977. 'They wouldn't have taken her seriously, those blokes. But it's not right, it's just not right, what happened. They thought they knew everything, those detectives – and they really didn't, did they?'

Gladys Coventry was not the only person to have witnessed something that related directly to the killings. Nor was she the only resident from whom detectives failed to take a statement. The wide brick-and-weatherboard that Hugh Parry-Jones and his family have lived in for the past thirty-one years provided another connection to the street's double homicide.

The Sellers family were living in 139 Easey Street when the murders occurred. Bob Sellers, now eighty-eight, was born there and raised his own family under the same roof. He and his wife and daughter were driving back from a holiday in Queensland that week, arriving home in the early hours of Thursday morning, 13 January 1977.

But his son, Peter, remained in Melbourne that summer. 'I was on holidays too – but to be honest, I wanted to go to the races,' the former track-work rider and apprentice jockey laughs.

The then 21-year-old didn't know Suzanne Armstrong or Susan Bartlett, but remembers them living in the street. 'They'd walk past and we'd say hi to them. They hadn't been there long, I know that. But they were quiet, kept to themselves.'

The night they were killed, just four doors away, a mate called Ray was staying with him. They were up late, talking and watching television. Peter will never forget what happened just after they had gone to bed. 'It's like it was yesterday. We'd just been watching tele and went to bed at about 2.30 am. My bedroom was at the front of the house and I'd just got into bed when I heard one door slam – like a front door. Then two car doors slammed and the car took off. That's what I heard, most likely the murderers leaving – and my mate the next morning, he said he heard it too.'

Two nights later, between 8.30 and 8.45 pm, Peter thought he heard his family arriving home and went outside to meet them. But it wasn't them. Instead, just down the road, he saw two men and a young woman standing at the edge of the bluestone lane.

'There was a blonde-haired guy and another one with darker hair, and a girl was with them,' he recalls. 'The blonde-haired guy kissed her on the cheek, then walked up the lane; she turned and walked towards Hoddle Street.'

Wondering where the bloke was going at that time of night, and knowing the lane ran into the small alley that led to his own backyard, Peter walked back through his house and into the yard to see if he was anywhere to be seen. He wasn't. Cindy, the family's labrador, was unfazed, not barking at all as they scouted her territory.

Peter's parents arrived home several hours later. He left for work as usual later that Thursday morning and it wasn't until the afternoon, when he picked up a copy of *The Herald*, that he realised something terrible had happened so close to his home. 'I got the paper, and it knocked the hell out of me.'

His mother told one of the police officers door-knocking in Easey Street that her son had something to tell them which could prove vital in the inquiry. 'Mum said the copper wrote my name down in his book and put a big asterisk next to it and told her they'd be back to talk with me. Forty-two years later, I haven't heard from them.' When the police officer who had spoken to his mother didn't return, Peter assumed they just weren't interested in what he had seen and heard over the two nights.

Peter said the friend who stayed at his house that Monday night – who has since passed away – was also willing to talk to police, once he knew about the murders. 'My thing is: why didn't they come back and see me?' For quite some time, he was more concerned that the killer – or killers – would come back.

Peter's question is a fair one, and can be broadened: why didn't detectives working this case in January 1977 knock on more doors in Easey Street?

If they were too stretched in terms of staff – with only sixteen detectives assigned to Victoria's Homicide Squad at that point – why weren't local police called in to assist? In fact, why wasn't Collingwood CIB involved in this investigation right from the outset? They would have had a deeper understanding of the suburb, its characters and possible 'persons of interest'.

Apparently, such collaboration rarely happened in that era, and only occurred if the lead detective instigated it. 'And there's detectives and there's detectives,' a former CIB chief remarked. 'No, Homicide seemed to do these things on their own. They'd knock on a certain number of doors, but they would have had so many murders on their plates – it wasn't like watching John Thaw [as Inspector Morse] driving round in his Jaguar, working on just one murder at a time.' This case was high-profile, but the Homicide Squad had finite resources and other murders to investigate.

About a week later, Peter Sellers walked past 147 Easey Street with his brother and father and saw the door was wide open. The house was in the process of being cleaned, but the blood in the hallway was still visible, even from the street. 'I reckon the blood was a foot from the front door,' he says.

Forty years on, with the cold case back in the news after police posted the million-dollar reward for information leading to the arrest of the killer, the Sellers family started discussing the murders again, and Peter's older sister convinced him he should call Crime Stoppers Victoria, to tell them what he had seen and heard all those years ago. 'To start with, I didn't know whether to or not – it was such a long time ago and everything, and they hadn't seemed very interested when it had just happened. But my sister hassled me. So I rang and I was on hold for ages, and I got really nervous,' Peter, now sixty-three, recollects. 'I don't know why, I obviously wasn't the murderer or anything ... but I was hanging on for so long.'

Finally getting through, he started to explain what had happened, but quickly got the feeling that they weren't interested. 'I got the impression they wanted a name,' he says now. 'And I couldn't give them a name, so they didn't want to talk to me all that much. In the end, they just kind of said "thank you" and that was it.'

He admits that he didn't get the chance to tell them the whole sequence of events, and never called back. In other words, he still hasn't given a proper statement to police.

This troubles him, because he believes the theory that seems to have stood the test of time – that just one man was involved in Susan Bartlett and Suzanne Armstrong's murders – isn't right. Having distinctly heard *two* car doors slam in the early hours of that Tuesday morning, Peter thinks police should consider the possibility that two people were at the scene. 'I've got no doubt whatsoever that there were two people involved. None whatsoever.'

This also makes sense to Robyn McKenzie, his sister. She feels it explains why such a 'tall, big girl' like Susan Bartlett was overpowered in the passageway. 'She was strong and tall and I could never understand how one guy could have done that, even with a knife.'

The Sellers have lived with a sense of frustration for decades, waiting for police to realise there was a possible witness they had missed. When Robyn persuaded her brother to call Crime

Stoppers, she was disappointed with the result. 'I pushed Peter to call,' she says. 'I said you have to, it's your duty to call them.' But 'they shrugged it off and said it wasn't relevant; apparently it didn't fit their timeline'.

Robyn remembers that police 'interrogated' her mother and father back in 1977 when they realised what time the family had arrived home. She says at that stage police believed the women had been killed on the Thursday morning, at around the time the Sellers returned. So, understandably, they were especially keen to talk to the owners of the car that matched the tyre marks in the lane. 'It wasn't very nice. They were just firing questions at us: "What time was it?" "What did you see?" That kind of thing.' It doesn't surprise her that an older woman such as Gladys Coventry would find a similar approach to questioning hard to deal with.

Robyn is also certain of something she saw from the back seat of the family car early on 13 January. 'It was just after 2.00 am in the morning, very early,' she says. 'And I absolutely remember we drove into the lane, before turning around [to park] in the street. And I noticed there were no lights on. I know people have said they saw the kitchen light was on, but when we were getting home, that house was dark.'

Her brother confirms that his sister has always maintained the house was 'completely dark' – and so too her father.

But Bob Sellers is derisive about some of the initial media coverage of the case, especially a statement attributed to him in *The Herald* published on the afternoon the bodies were discovered. In it, he seemed to suggest that Armstrong and Bartlett were loud 'party girls'.

'That's rubbish, I didn't say that at all,' he grumbles. 'You'd say hello to them in the street and they hadn't been there for long. They were nice girls. Nice girls.

'In those times, everyone played out in the street until it got dark. In those days, the doors and windows were open to get some air in. Now, you're a prisoner in your own house.'

Bob now lives in the curator's house on the grounds of Collingwood Football Club, and says he remembers driving his car into the side lane at 'ten past two' that Thursday morning. 'Those laneways were for the "dirt man" to come and take the pans away,' he adds.

He knew Mrs Coventry, but they never discussed the murders, so she never told him about what she saw the night they occurred. 'No, I never spoke to her about it ... she was a bit of a boozer, I know that much. But that's a long time ago now.'

His daughter remembers the family used to call her 'a funny old bird – but that doesn't mean she didn't see someone in that house that night'.

Despite their street's sudden notoriety, the Sellers never considered it unsafe. 'We never suspected anyone in the street – we knew all of them,' Bob Sellers says. Still, he can't forget the impact the women's deaths had on his old stomping ground. 'We had thrill-seekers driving past and pointing at the house at the time, kids hanging out of car windows pointing and laughing it up.' He and his family found this behaviour unsettling. 'It was the talking point of Easey Street, that's for sure. But they were nice girls. Nice girls.'

CHAPTER 10

THE NEWSPAPERS

FOR SERIOUS JOURNALISTS in 1977, one of the most compelling beats to have was working 'police rounds': following the major squads as they investigated baffling, high-profile crimes. Many of the nation's best reporters did a stint in this arena. It wasn't for the faint-hearted: it required discipline, the gift of the gab, the ability to file stories quickly and accurately, and, to a degree, the knowledge to work both sides of the story: coppers and crims.

In Melbourne, it also meant working cheek-by-jowl in a shoebox office in Russell Street Police Headquarters, opposite the imposing Melbourne Magistrates Court. A grisly news story such as the Easey Street double murder provided an intriguing opportunity for some of the city's high-profile crime journalists. From Thursday morning, 13 January 1977, there was no bigger story for the next forty-eight hours – and it's instructive to note how it was told.

For the first few days after the women's bodies were discovered, the news coverage was straightforward, reporting on the details of the crime that had occurred and describing what police were doing at the house and around the neighbourhood, tapping into what senior detectives were saying publicly, to keep pace with the investigation.

Gradually, journalists fanned wider as they tried to build a portrait of the women's lives. Decades before social media provided almost instantaneous connection to friends and family, this could prove challenging. Not everyone trapped in sudden tragedy wanted to deal with the print or broadcast media, and it was still possible to avoid intrusive requests for interviews or photographs.

At the time, there was no writer more prolific than Ron Connelly, chief police reporter for *The Herald*. The city's afternoon broadsheet would start rolling out around midday, and if a story was big enough, continue with updated editions throughout the afternoon. One banner headline ran across four editions of the paper that Thursday – '2 WOMEN KNIFED TO DEATH' shouted the city edition, with the number '2' being changed to 'TWO' for the next three, as his crisp, factual reporting added levels of detail to the ugly tale.

'Police launched a man-hunt in Collingwood today after the bodies of two women were found in a house in Easey Street,' the article began.

> Detectives said both of the women, aged about 25, had been stabbed to death. They said both had multiple stab wounds. Police were called to the single-fronted painted brick home soon after 10am. A woman reported finding the two bodies only minutes before. Detectives said one of the victims was found lying in a bedroom. The second body was in a hallway a short distance away.

> Detectives believe the women were killed last night. When police arrived at the house today they found a note pinned to the front door. The note was to remind the occupants of the house that their dog had been found wandering in the street.
>
> Detectives say they could find no motive for the murders. A small boy, aged about two, was carried from the house by a policewoman soon after the bodies were discovered.

It was classic on-the-spot reporting, what would today be called 'developing news', no doubt filed from a telephone box to a copy-taker at *The Herald*'s office.

The second edition included lurid new facts: police had found a blood-soaked towel in a playground area in nearby Wellington Street, just a few hundred metres away from the house; and, more chillingly, police said the woman in the bedroom 'had been attacked':

> She was naked from the waist down and a skivvy was pulled up around her neck. She had numerous knife wounds on her chest and chin. Police said the second victim was fully clothed and had apparently tried to flee from the attacker. They said she had a large stab wound in the back. Blood was spattered around the hallway and the bedroom. There were smears on the wall which police believe were left when the second woman tried to hold on for support as she slumped dying to the floor.

This level of detail would rarely be given to reporters now, at least not so quickly, and outside a courtroom setting. It is testament to Ron Connelly's journalistic skills that he was able to gather so much information so fast, and illustrates, as well, the rapport that reporters 'back in the day' often developed with the detectives on the job.

Four photographs made it into this edition of the paper: a shot of the house, another of the note about the dog, a smaller shot of Ilona Stevens with the dog and a picture of neighbours talking to police in the street. There was also a small map, pinpointing Easey Street's location, between well-known thoroughfares Alexandra Parade and Johnston Street.

In the final edition that day, the veteran crime reporter wrote that 'detectives ... believed they were looking for a crazed sex killer', a few paragraphs later adding that Susan Bartlett's brother, Martin, had been told of his sister's death 'when he rang the house at noon'. The first two photos of the women to be published in the media appear on this front page, with Suzanne Armstrong holding her baby son close for the camera. Connelly also recorded police correcting their estimate of the women's time of death: 'Police believe the two women could have been murdered as early as last Monday.'

Over a few hours, the newshound had vividly outlined the murder scene, developed a narrative around the killings and fed the city information about the early police investigation. It was an extraordinary example of the era's 'rolling news' style of coverage. In the same way that television news channels now cover 'developing' news, the city's major afternoon daily had quickly revealed the horror of what occurred inside the house and how the police were responding.

The next morning, *The Herald*'s sister tabloid, *The Sun*, focused on the fact that sixteen-month-old Greg could have been alone in the 'murder house' for 'possibly 48 hours after his mother and her friend were stabbed to death'. Inside, Tony Wilson's report went wider, trying to capture the women's personalities by incorporating comments from friends and neighbours – including from Barry Woodard's sister, Margaret Chilcott. 'Neighbours in Easy [sic] Street said they had not really had time to get to know the two, who had been in the house only seven weeks. One woman saw them walking their dog and going to the milk bar opposite their house.' The article highlighted that the girls had been friends since their school days in Benalla, and that Sue was a well-liked, dedicated teacher. Suzanne 'was devoted to her son and had been battling financially to support him', Chilcott said.

The double homicide was the lead story in *The Age* that morning too, and their investigative team pushed even harder, following up the clue left in the note on the kitchen table. Reporters Gerry Carman and Michael Gordon found 'Barry', not long after police had tracked him down. 'The boyfriend of one of two young women stabbed to death in a Collingwood house on Tuesday visited the house on Wednesday night and left without discovering the killings,' they wrote. 'The bodies of Suzanne Armstrong, 27, an unmarried mother, and Susan Bartlett, 28, a school teacher, lay in pools of blood where the man stood. The boyfriend, Mr Barry Woodard, went to the house with his brother and left a note in the kitchen after assuming the women were out.'

Again, it was a textbook example of robust crime writing, as Carman and Gordon relayed the boyfriend's statement, allowing readers to draw their own conclusions. The 31-year-old shearer told the journalists he had been to the house with his 24-year-old brother Henry at about 8.30 pm on Wednesday – about twelve hours before their bodies were found:

> 'I last saw Susan at midday on Sunday and had not been able to contact her, despite repeated attempts on the telephone,' Mr Woodard said. 'I rang her again from my sister's place at 7 pm on Wednesday, but there was no reply. I decided to go to the house with Henry. We noticed a note pinned to the front door but got no response to knocking and calling out, so we walked around the side lane and entered the half-open back gate. The kitchen light was on. Henry left a note under an ash tray on the kitchen table saying: "Ring Barry as soon as you get home" and we left,' Mr Woodard said.

The note didn't say what Barry Woodard described at all, of course; it was just a name and a number, rather than a complete message. But this fact was never corrected by police, or in later media reports.

Across Melbourne, speculation about Barry's and Henry's presence in the house quickly became a key point of discussion around the case. There was one question that was raised: why did these two men, so keen to find Suzanne Armstrong, go no further into the house, and not even look up the hallway? Perhaps Greg had cried himself to sleep by then and was making no noise. But having been so worried they could not reach their friend, and having gone to such effort to connect with her, why didn't at least one of them check through the rooms?

Gerry Carman and Michael Gordon did not pose these questions directly to Woodard. But they did delve deeper in their second piece on the case, headlined 'Violent Death Ended a Christmas Love Story'. It revealed an interesting detail:

> Roving shearer Barry Woodard clasped his shaking hands yesterday as he told his story. It was Christmas Day when he first met Suzanne Armstrong, the young woman he believed he would marry. Yesterday she was dead, savagely stabbed. 'And I stood only six metres from her body on Wednesday night, not knowing she was there,' he said. 'I'm numb, my stomach is in a knot, but I don't think it's hit me yet. I never thought anything like this would happen to me.'
>
> ...
>
> 'When the announcer on the telly said two women had been murdered in Collingwood and the kid had been taken to hospital, I felt a funny feeling in my stomach. We had been trying to ring the house for three days but when Margaret dialled yesterday a policeman immediately answered the phone. I got on but couldn't talk. They came and picked me up for questioning at Russell Street headquarters. They even took my fingerprints, but I didn't mind. I had nothing to hide. I was crying.'

He told the journalists his brother Henry, a farmhand from Seymour, had introduced the two of them. 'Sue's sister Gayle is going with Henry ... it looked as if we were keeping them in the family.' Woodard confirmed that Suzanne had recently returned from Greece, where she had given birth to her son. The shearer made the odd comment that the 'Yugoslav father of her child' would not marry her because she would not conform with a custom that women should not cross their legs. 'She wouldn't go along with it. It's crazy,' he said. Woodard also tried to summarise his feelings for Armstrong. 'I think I would have asked her to marry me ... I really loved her, and I believe she did the same.'

The pair had only been out three times, but he evidently felt their bond was strong.

By the end of the week, Melbournians knew what Suzanne and Sue had been forced to endure on the last night of their lives. Sue had been stabbed 'at least 40 times', Ron Connelly reported, Suzanne 'more than 25 times'. Both figures were incorrect, as it turned out – but the morning newspapers were soon quoting the head of the Homicide Squad describing the killings as 'one of the most brutal sex crimes in Victorian history'. 'Whoever stabbed these women is a very, very sick person – a maniac type,' *The Sun* reported Inspector Noel Jubb as saying. 'Detectives are looking through police files on all known sex offenders. We can't afford to have this killer loose for long because he might strike again.'

The Age was only slightly more circumspect, with Gerry Carman revealing that detectives were following two key leads: 'They do not want their information released at this stage as one involves evidence taken from the Collingwood house where the women's bodies were found. The other involves a man with a history of violent rape.' Like many of these early reports, this article included factual errors: it wrongly stated that Sue was stabbed forty-three times and Suzanne twenty-five times, and both were raped. These 'facts' were later corrected.

According to this report, a team of twenty-five detectives had been assigned to the case, but they still did not know if the man they were hunting knew the women. Police had been back at the house on Friday, searching for clues. 'Besides speaking to people in the neighbourhood, they interviewed six men at Russell St Headquarters. All were cleared. They were also going through a contact book and personal letters taken from the house.'

The reporter noted that a high-profile police source had told him the Homicide Squad were 'floundering a bit' in their search for solid suspects. This revelation, coming only a few days after the women's bodies had been discovered, must have concerned the immediate families and many in the community.

Over the following days, more details emerged. Inspector Jubb suggested the 'frenzied nature' of the attack indicated that only one man was responsible. He said a sharp weapon, like a breadknife, was used in heavy, rapid thrusts to inflict very deep wounds. 'Both women were struck with tremendous ferocity.'

A day later, a different blade became the focus of media attention – a knife in a sheath found just a few hundred metres away from the 'murder house' at Collingwood's Victoria Park Station. *The Age* described the discovery as the 'one of the strongest leads yet in the search to the Easey Street sex killer', noting that forensic scientists had found blood samples on the handle of the knife that matched the blood group of one of the victims. 'The knife was … discovered just 90 minutes after the last known person to see the women alive left their house,' journalist Michael Gordon wrote.

This seemed a promising development, and was certainly one that would have attracted the attention of the Melburnians who were following the investigation closely.

But the evidence that this knife was the murder weapon proved flimsy, at best. 'There are no blood samples on the knife to match the blood grouping of Miss Bartlett. The knife had been wiped clean. Scientists found blood samples inside its brown plastic handle. The blood group found ... was Group A, the same as Suzanne Armstrong's blood type. There was no trace of Miss Bartlett's Group O. Both blood groups are fairly common.'

The knife was soon discounted by one Inspector Jubb because it had been found 'too soon' after the killings. At least, that's what *The Sun* reported on Monday 17 January 1977. But that didn't stop the salacious media interest. Three days later, *The Herald* led its morning edition with a question: 'DID THIS KILL 2 GIRLS?' alongside a photograph of the knife and its sheath. The weekly *Melbourne Times* honed in on a particularly disturbing detail. 'Police believe ... the killer spent some time inside the house before leaving. It is believed he was attempting to wash off bloodstains', said its front-page piece.

Chief Inspector Don Plant, metropolitan crime coordinator, warned women living alone to keep their doors locked at night. 'With a sex killer like this at large, there is always a danger of a repeat attack,' he said. He had revisited the women's house in Easey Street the day before, 'checking in case anything had been missed, but we found nothing new'.

He appealed to Collingwood residents to come forward if they saw anyone acting suspiciously on the previous Monday night or early Tuesday: 'As the murdered women's home is only 400 m from the Victoria Park railway station, it is just possible the killer may have escaped by train and been seen by local residents or passersby.' The chief inspector also appealed to 'dry-cleaners or anyone with information that blood-stained clothing had been laundered since the attack': 'Not only could there have been blood stains on the killer's clothes, but he may also have had scratches on his face.'

These pleas for public assistance seemed to reveal no useful information to police – at least, nothing that has ever been revealed publicly.

As the days went by, journalists soon found they had little new to report. It appeared that the police were struggling to come up with more clues, evidence or suspects – anything much at all. With no news on a suspect, the daily newspapers rehashed information already reported, with headlines designed to shock: 'Sex Killer Bathed in House', 'Surrender Plea to Sex Killer'. They were lurid, but led nowhere.

One reassuring detail did emerge from the coverage: Gregory, who was treated for dehydration after his 48-hour ordeal in his cot, had been placed in the custody of his uncle, Terry Armstrong, Suzanne's younger brother. The cattle-truck driver and father of two arrived from Benalla to collect the toddler from the Allambie Reception Centre in Burwood days after Suzanne's death.

In this most agonising of circumstances, members of the women's families assumed the temporary celebrity status of the publicly grief-stricken – thrust under a garish spotlight. For days, they formed the core of the city's daily conversation. Their pain was widely dissected, as was the horrific nature of the murders that now formed their immutable bond.

A week after the women's bodies had been recovered, there was another jarring visit to the Easey Street house. But this one was sanctioned by detectives. Suzanne Armstrong's father and Sue Bartlett's brother were allowed to remove their loved ones' belongings. Tess Lawrence, one of *The Herald's* leading columnists, was permitted to wander up the hall and through the bedrooms as Bill Armstrong and Martin Bartlett packed up the women's personal items. She even managed to talk to them briefly.

'I know two wrongs don't make a right,' said Suzanne's father. 'But please, he must be found, the man who did it must be found. She was a wonderful girl. Oh, wonderful and independent. Did everything herself. Always did. Strong-minded. A strong will.

'I remember when we first brought her home. Her first day, you know? She just sat up and had a bit of a look at the world, as if to say, *so this is it, eh? This is where you've brought me* ... She's always done well, could have got a job anywhere. Well, she travelled the world twice. She mixes in anywhere.'

In the kitchen, the journalist watched as Sue Bartlett's brother found the soda syphon he'd given his sister for Christmas a couple of weeks earlier. 'If only people would realise what it means to us to find whoever did it,' Martin told her. 'Not only for our peace of mind, but also for theirs. It would help the community and we would all rest a bit easier – especially women. He's out there, living an existence. If someone suspects anything or anyone, will they please go to the police. It doesn't matter how insignificant they think it is.'

The media glare on the families did not last long. With no new developments, within the next week journalistic attention began to drift away from this tragedy, although *The Sunday Press* tried to stir things up by publishing a long interview with Barry Woodard. It was the most intimate coverage of the double homicide to date, with Suzanne's suitor proving detailed in his responses to questions.

Woodard was expansive about how he had been treated when questioned by detectives the day the two bodies were found, and about his relationship with Suzanne. 'I was grilled at one stage by eight detectives, who kept me in a room and just fired questions at me from behind and in front,' he told British-born journalist Richard Shears. 'I was sick to my stomach because the girl that I loved had been murdered, yet I was the No. 1 suspect. I had my first meal – bacon and eggs – in two days this morning. I've been in pieces over this terrible business.

'I hope … my name will be cleared completely. I've heard the whispers, but I take no notice of them. All I know is that my future with Suzanne has been destroyed.'

He recounted how he had called Suzanne for the first time just a couple of weeks earlier, to ask if she would go out with him. 'It was Christmas Day that Henry suggested I ring Suzanne. So I simply telephoned and said, "Would you like to go out on a blind date?" She giggled a bit down the phone and said that yes, she would. We arranged it for the following weekend. I picked her up and we drove to a rodeo 30 miles north of Bendigo.

'I took my camera along with me and I was going to get some pictures taken of us, but can you believe it, I forgot to put film in! But we had a marvellous time. We went to the local pub in the evening and had a few drinks and then we stayed overnight at my brother's place. She struck me right away as being a very kind, considerate person. She offered to drive my car from Bendigo to Melbourne because she thought I was feeling tired.'

He said that after they had dinner with his sister and her family in Northcote the night before she died, 'we took the portable TV out onto the lawn and had a few drinks'. 'That was the first and last time we were all together like that. By now I was very much in love with Suzanne and I felt good about the plans we had made to get married over the next few months. It may all sound very quick, but these things happen.'

Woodard also went into greater detail about how he and his brother had visited the house in Easey Street that Wednesday and saw nothing untoward. 'The impression we gained was that no one was in, but we went around the back anyway,' he told *The Sunday Press*. 'The gate was half open, and so was the back door, with the kitchen light on. I called Suzanne's name from the doorway, but there was no reply. People, I know, have asked why I didn't find the bodies. The simple reason is that I didn't go into the house. Henry wanted to go in and look around but I said, "No, it's not our place." And if they came back and find [sic] us wandering around inside, it wouldn't look very nice, would it?'

His guard came down as he talked to his Fleet Street–trained inquisitor. He claimed he rang again the following morning, without success. His brother-in-law, Max Chilcott, was by now suspicious that something was wrong, even speculating to Margaret that it would be horrible if the women had met with foul play.

'Not long afterwards, around 10.30am, there was a flash on the television saying that two girls had been murdered in Collingwood. I just felt myself go cold. I immediately rang the house and this time, for the first time in days, the phone was engaged. Strangely, I had a strong feeling of relief. But I had read it all wrong. "Thank heavens for that," I remember saying to Margaret. "They're home."

'In fact, it was Margaret who rang again five minutes later, and she looked across at me and said, "A detective has answered." Margaret then asked the detective, "They aren't the two girls who were murdered, were they?" And I could tell by her face that they were.'

The police quickly picked up Barry Woodard, his brother and sister, and drove them to Russell Street, where he said he was placed in a room alone. 'The questions came from all directions and I got totally confused about where I was on such-and-such a night and what time it was and so on. In a way, I'm grateful about that questioning because it was very intense and then they released me. At least it proved I was telling the truth about everything, because if I did have anything to hide that questioning would have tripped me up without a doubt.'

He said he didn't know where his life was heading now, and expressed an interest in taking 'the little boy' into his care, but supposed he would stay with family. It seemed strange that he did not use Greg's name. But to be fair, he must have felt under enormous stress.

The Sunday Press also included an update on the portrait the police were building of the 'breadknife maniac', insisting that police were convinced only one man was responsible for the stabbing wounds inflicted on the women.

And that was it, pretty much, for the intense mainstream media coverage. Less than two weeks after they died, the women dropped out of the daily newspaper headlines. As willing as Melbourne's most experienced crime journalists were to follow the investigation, the police were struggling to come up with new directions.

After Shears' interview with Woodard it was left to weekly tabloids to generate new angles; many of them did their own reporting and turned up new, controversial information. *Truth*, the self-proclaimed 'top-selling weekly paper' in Victoria, was keen to capitalise on the interest the case had generated – and it did so with an 'exclusive interview' with staff member Ilona Stevens, the neighbour of the two women. 'MY DAY OF HORROR – EXCLUSIVE – Girl Next Door Tells' was the banner that ran in such large typeface across the cover there was only room for one paragraph next to Ilona's photo. 'The horror of that morning will haunt me for the rest of my life. I keep thinking it could have been my girlfriend and I [sic] who lay dead and mutilated.'

There was an even more gruesome banner: 'BLOOD SOAKED TROUSERS CLUE' ran above the article from legendary *Truth* reporter Jack Ayling. A pair of blood-soaked pants had been handed in to a suburban dry-cleaning agency less than a mile from Easey Street. 'The trousers were dry-cleaned and collected two hours before this edition of *Truth* went to press on Thursday,' the report said. The pants had remained at the cleaners for nine days. The female manager of the cleaning agency had asked the customer how they had become so badly stained. The man said he had cut his hand, but she told *Truth* all she could see was a slight nick on one finger: 'It looked to me as if no more than one layer of skin had been penetrated.' The woman, the paper noted, 'did not attach any sinister significance to the bloodstains or associate them with the Collingwood murders because the bodies were not discovered until Thursday morning, January 13'.

A week later, the paper claimed to have another lead about a 'vital clue'. According to journalist Ian Dougall, a middle-aged man in a 'disturbed condition', with blood dripping from his hands, had sought treatment at St Vincent's Hospital in Fitzroy on 10 January 1977, only hours after the murders. And just a few kilometres from Easey Street. The man had apparently fled when asked for his name and address.

'Detective Senior Sergeant Alf Oldfield told *Truth* that police had ... interviewed the nurse at St Vincent's Hospital and were hopeful it could lead to the identity of the killer,' the paper reported. 'The nurse told [them] she didn't place any significance on the man fleeing from the hospital because the bodies were not found until Thursday, January 13.'

Of course, there was no CCTV footage to record the hospital visit – CCTV wouldn't come into use until several years later. So this became another potential lead that fell flat.

Truth's fourth and final exclusive on the 'Collingwood murders' again focused on staffer Ilona Stevens, who was still living at 149 Easey Street. 'PROWLER IN DEATH HOUSE', screamed the main headline. '2 am terror for lone girl next door.' Ilona denies that there was ever any prowler, or that she was even interviewed for this 'follow up'. As many who worked for the paper recall, that was the way *Truth* rolled. Perhaps the weekly tabloid was trying to keep public pressure on police as the investigation seemed to lose steam? Or was it simply a garish attempt to sell papers?

One thing would have been obvious, even to the casual follower of the case: the lack of new information on the murders, given the close working relationship reporters at the major daily newspapers had with detectives at the time, could only mean there were no new details coming through to the police. If this was troubling to many in the community, it must have been deeply alarming for the families.

Three months later, *The Sunday Press* had one last report: a front-page 'flier' headline announced '$7000 for Gregory, Baby of Murder', pointing to Richard Shears' update inside, on pages two and three. A concerned Melbourne barrister who had been following the case had set up a trust fund for the toddler, and it stood at $7000. This included $2000 from a fundraiser held at the Normanby Hotel in Clifton Hill. But Shears' focus was checking in with Gregory's 'new mother', Suzanne Armstrong's sister, Gayle.

The initial disbelief of what had happened on 10 January that year had passed for this family; so too the intense grief of the funeral. 'Now all Gayle feels is an emptiness because there are questions that need to be answered and no one has come forward to help,' the report said. 'But she smiles when she talks about Gregory. She runs a hand through his long hair as he plays around her feet. "He's very happy here. He'll grow up happy too, because I intend to see it that way."

'"I have heard through a mutual friend that Gregory's father, who lives on a Greek island, is intending to get custody. But I and the rest of the family want him to stay here – and I think a lot of people will be in sympathy with us."'

Richard Shears was not as successful in prising information

from the Homicide Squad. Despite detectives interviewing 'dozens of people whose names appear in a diary found in the house', some more than once, no clear suspect had emerged. 'The trail is a bit cold at the moment,' Inspector Noel Jubb confessed. 'But that doesn't mean we have given up our efforts. Every minor lead that comes our way is being carefully followed up.' The article continued, 'Baby Gregory, who plays happily on a bicycle in a garden in the country, will be two in August. Police and the two girls' families hope that by his third birthday, his mother's killer will have been captured, convicted and jailed.'

Of course, that didn't happen. There would be no neat endings in this saga.

Six months after Sue and Suzanne died, as Greg celebrated his second birthday with his extended family, the man who had murdered his mother remained free. Forty-two birthdays later, this still holds true.

CHAPTER 11
THE SUSPECTS

DESPITE THE CLOSE relationships many journalists had with police across the force, detectives could not confirm the leads they were pursuing, not to mention what they were thinking about the Easey Street crime site and the possible profile of the killer, without compromising the investigation or libelling suspects. But from the start of this investigation, the city's senior crime reporters knew of the two men 'in the frame'. Within days, most journalists working on Melbourne's daily newspapers were on to this angle, too.

Barry Woodard had caught police attention in the first few days of the inquiry. Those close to the victim are always investigated in homicide cases. But, just hours after the Homicide Squad arrived at Easey Street, their attention fell on another suspect, someone they felt they knew much better. It was a crime reporter – the male journalist who had stayed the night at Ilona Stevens' place, in the house next door to the crime scene.

John Grant was a well-known writer in Melbourne at the time, who had been covering the 'police beat' for years, and detectives quickly became focused on where he claimed to have been at the time of the murders: sleeping on a couch next door. They also believed his job gave him knowledge of the forensic procedures of the time.

Like the salacious, knuckles bared–style tabloid he wrote for, 'Grunter' and many of his colleagues were proud of the fact they could work both sides of the 'crime beat', hanging out with police sources one night, criminal contacts the next. 'Crime rounds were different then,' a former colleague recollects. 'The reporters "consorted" – they'd hang out with crooked coppers and crims. They had to, to get the yarns.'

This kind of work did not come naturally or appeal to everyone, and doing it well required a rugged disposition. Grant had one, and was a polarising personality within journalistic circles. He certainly lived up to the stereotype of a 'police roundsman' of the era: a big-talking, big-drinking journo, perhaps living a little too close to the edge of the criminal networks he wrote about.

Back then, colleagues either enjoyed his company or steered clear of him, and even now they still choose their words carefully when discussing him. At the very least, he was 'a character', known for his knock-the-door-down type of journalism. Much of the apprehension around Grant grew from what happened in Easey Street once it became apparent that he had stayed in the adjoining house on the night of the murders.

John Grant was not in a relationship with either Ilona Stevens or Janet Powell, and had never visited their home before. But after drinking and talking into the early hours of that Tuesday morning, Ilona had suggested he stay over on their couch rather than find his way home.

The trio insisted to police that they heard and saw nothing unusual that night. This was possible: the two cottages shared a common wall, with identical hallways running side by side, but the bedrooms and lounge rooms were on opposite sides of the properties, which meant all three at 149 were sleeping against the far wall, several metres away from the violence taking place next door.

Still, investigators could not ignore the coincidence of the reporter being in the wrong place for a second time in the space of two years. On 1 July 1975, he had been in a small group with a woman named Julie Ann Garciacelay the night the young American disappeared from her apartment in North Melbourne.

The nineteen-year-old had invited three men back to the apartment she shared with her sister Gail, one of them Grant, the other two notorious figures well known to police. Garciacelay has never been seen since. So it was hardly surprising that he was considered a key suspect in the early days of the Easey Street investigation.

He was one of the first men police interviewed at the Russell Street headquarters, and their questioning lasted an entire day. The session was unrelentingly tough; as one now retired detective has confided, 'they didn't miss him'. In other words, they did not go easy on him, or treat him with any professional courtesy.

Grant maintained his innocence throughout the interview and has continued to do so for the past four decades. He was also cleared of involvement by DNA testing.

Yet great damage was done to his reputation in the immediate days and long years after the double homicide. It wasn't fair, but in Melbourne's tight media circle, misinformation about him was rife: he had been waiting at the door of the murdered women's house when police arrived, the stories went – and he found the murder weapon just up the road! None of this was true, of course, but that didn't stop it from being repeated. For years. The fact that he worked for *Truth* was just icing on the gloaters' cake.

Peter Hiscock, the young detective who attended the murder scene and now works as a private investigator, pulls no punches about his assessment of the reporter at the time. 'I thought it had to be John Grant,' he admits. 'How many crime reporters could be in the wrong spot twice? I got it wrong, I admit that. He's been cleared twice now.'

On 11 April 2018, nineteen-year-old Julie Ann Garciacelay was officially deemed a murder victim. 'Despite there being no evidence as to the exact circumstance and cause of Ms Garciacelay's death, her death was the result of homicide,' Victoria's state coroner, Sara Hinchey, declared.

As crime stories went, it wasn't big news, coming forty-three years after the young American had disappeared. So it didn't warrant front-page headlines; indeed, only one of Melbourne's daily newspapers reported it, and even then, the story was relegated to page twelve of the print edition. But the ramifications of Ms Hinchey's ruling were dramatic, and not just for the Garciacelay case. Homicide detectives could now review the files, which had so far been treated as a missing-person case, and the details of the night that involved the three men at Julie's apartment. One of the three, John Joseph Power, had always been considered 'the real deal, the real *bad* deal' by at least one lawyer who knew him.

When police dusted off Garciacelay's missing-person file, new attention could be focused on the possibility that one of Grant's professional 'contacts' had been involved in the Easey Street murders. One or two detectives might have long suspected this, but no proof had ever been found.

In 2018, the Coroner's Court was told that the young woman from California had been working as a library reference clerk at Southdown Press, the Murdoch-owned publisher that later became Pacific Magazines, in Melbourne's La Trobe Street. *The Truth* and *The Australian* newspapers were printed there, and on the day of her disappearance, Julie had spoken to Grant and two of his 'associates' when they were in the library: one, a former fairground boxer, Rhys 'Tommy' Collins; the other, career criminal John Joseph Power. As *The Age* reported, the coroner heard that while in the library on 1 July 1975, the trio had drawn the American, who was just a week shy of her twentieth birthday, into a conversation about opening a soul-food restaurant.

Keen to extend her social circle in Melbourne, having moved to Australia only eight months earlier, Julie organised a get-together with the men for later that night, back at her apartment. The block where she lived wasn't far from where she worked, in Canning Street, North Melbourne.

> Collins and Grant came over with another man, John Joseph Powers [sic], who had been acquitted of murdering a woman three years earlier and would later be jailed for 30 years over a shooting, armed robberies and the vicious 1992 rape of a 19-year-old.
>
> The men said Ms Garciacelay left the flat at 10.30 pm to make a call at a public phone box for her sister, Gail, who was

> at a friend's in Kew and had asked her to call in sick for her on her behalf. Ms Garciacelay never came home, the men said. Gail Garciacelay reported her sister missing at 4 pm the following day after coming home to find she had not showed up for work at Southdown Press.
>
> She also reportedly found a blood-soaked towel and her sister's underwear on the floor. Police would find a piece of paper with a phone number left by Gail, and money to make the call, inside the flat, while Gail's supervisor told police they never received a phone call from her sister that night either.

Contemporary crime journalists in Melbourne had been waiting for this mystery to come before the Coroner's Court for three years, after it was revealed in 2015 that the brief was being prepared. In a statement at that time, police confirmed their belief that Julie Ann 'is deceased'.

Over the preceding four decades, police had come to know the details of her disappearance and her family well. A talented pianist, she had come to Melbourne to be with a 'homesick' Gail Garciacelay, and the two young women had planned to return to the United States before Christmas that year.

Detectives knew, too, that significant items were missing from the sisters' North Melbourne flat: a carving knife, a black cape and $125 in cash. Over the years, they had also reportedly been given information about where her body was dumped that night in 1975, though it has still not been found.

While police ranked John Joseph Power a serious suspect in this young woman's disappearance from the outset, no move was made to bring him in for questioning. One reason for this could have been the complaint he had made to the Beach Inquiry, which was underway at the time, looking into allegations of misconduct against members of the Victoria Police Force.

Power had alleged that 'certain members of the Homicide Squad had conspired together with a view to having him wrongfully charged with the murder of a Mrs Rosa Rento, in the hope that they might have him convicted of that crime, and put out of circulation for the greater part of his life'. He claimed that he was arrested and charged with murder despite 'there being no evidence against him whatsoever, apart from a three year old motive he may have had to cause harm to the Rento family, said to exist because some three years previously Mrs. Rento's juvenile son had attempted to interfere with Power's infant daughter – at least so Power thought'.

The Beach inquiry provided validation to these allegations. It recorded that, at his trial, it was proved beyond doubt that the gun 'identified ... as the murder weapon had in fact been in the possession of the Police for some 6 weeks prior to the shooting'.

'How did it come about that this regrettable situation occurred?' the report asked.

> It occurred, the evidence before the Board suggests, because certain Police are content to do deals with informers rather than undertake the tedium of proper investigative work to solve crimes. Whilst the failure of the Police in this case does not fall within the same category of behaviour of those Police who find it easier to fabricate Records of Interview than make

> proper investigation into crime, it nevertheless justifies the strongest criticism.

If a strange sense of 'due process' protected John Power from further police attention through the mid to late 1970s, it worked in his favour again decades later, when a court order prevented him from being questioned about Julie Ann Garciacelay's disappearance, due to a health condition. According to a report in *The Age* in July 2015, he was on parole in 2002 when police alleged he met an escort near his housing-commission unit in Broadmeadows. They claim the woman told him she would only stay for forty-five minutes, not a full hour. He allegedly grabbed the woman and threatened her with a knife, before trying to gag her. She escaped and ran to a nearby house. His lawyer argued successfully that 'Power was dying of a heart condition and should not be questioned by police'. This applied to both the matter in question and, by extension, the Garciacelay case. But Power lived until July 2012, dying at the age of seventy-one.

Fifteen years after Julie Ann Garciacelay disappeared, police put out a public appeal for information. John Grant made a brief comment to a colleague that he had been 'to hell and back' since being linked to the murder. 'We went over there for a drink and that was it,' the former crime writer was reported to have said. 'She went away and we got tired of waiting and left ... I would like to see the whole thing solved too, of course. Get some peace for me, for everybody.'

It was an inelegant, gruff statement. Grant has never been willing to give a fuller account on the public record of what happened the night Garciacelay went missing – including his claim to police that he went home early that night, leaving her with Power and boxer Tommy Collins. He also declined to discuss either case for this book.

A decade ago, two detectives visited veteran journalist Adrian Tame to test part of Grant's statement to police: that on the night of Graciacelay's disappearance, the reporter had rung him and asked if he could take a taxi home, before grabbing a taxi docket from the office on the way. Tame was the news editor at *Truth* at the time and so would have been the one to approve such a request from a reporter. 'They came all the way to see me here in central Victoria [to inquire] if John had asked me if he could take a taxi home – but I couldn't remember if he had or not,' he says. The detectives also tried to persuade him to be 'wired up' to talk to his old colleague about the case. Adrian Tame refused to be involved. It is understood, too, that detectives asked John Grant to visit John Joseph Power in jail to see if he knew where the young woman's body could be found.

Those who know the former *Truth* reporter say the attempt to set up his old 'crim contact' was extraordinarily difficult for him to take on board. Yet if John Power had admitted involvement in Julie Ann Garciacelay's disappearance, it might also have led to his being questioned over the deaths of Susan Bartlett and Suzanne Armstrong. Some semblance of the peace John Grant is still so desperate to find could perhaps have extended to their families, as well as to Garciacelay's.

This is not to say, of course, that John Joseph Power would have admitted anything. It is simply speculation about where events could have led.

Where was the former gun-shop owner and member of the Painters and Dockers Union on the night of 10 January 1977? It remains unclear. He wasn't in jail, so police investigating the Easey Street murders must have looked into his movements, given their strong interest in Grant. But it seems that Power was not on their original list of suspects.

Another intriguing point: as detectives worked on both cases, staring at the photos of Julie Ann Garciacelay and the 'two Sues', did it occur to them how similar the three looked? Suzanne and Julie in particular – they shared long, brown hair and pale complexions.

Perhaps this was just another coincidence, like the bloodied towel left on the couch at both homicide scenes and the presence of underwear on the floors.

But perhaps, perhaps ... John Power somehow knew where John Grant was that night in January 1977. Maybe he had followed Grant and Ilona Stevens, without Grant's knowledge, to 149 Easey Street and noticed the two women and the little boy next door, or at least the young woman reading in bed, in the front room of her home.

Then again, what of Rhys 'Tommy' Collins? Could he have been involved in killing three women? Australia's welterweight champion in 1963, the former fairground boxer was more than accomplished in the ring, notching up twenty-seven victories in his career, eleven of them 'knockouts'. But he was also a 'two-up' operator known to police through a series of comparatively minor criminal convictions. One source who knew the former boxing champ, who died in 1998, claimed Collins was in a relationship with Garciacelay when she went missing in 1975, although there is no evidence of this.

Could Collins have been trailing John Grant for some reason two years later, when he and Ilona Stevens returned to Collingwood after work? Ilona can't remember seeing anyone hanging around in the street when they arrived home. She is adamant, too, that her colleague never mentioned John Power or Tommy Collins in conversation, either at work or socially. They didn't share a close friendship. 'We were just co-workers who were mates,' she says. 'He could have been a younger brother – that was the relationship.'

Ilona insists that Grant did not know the girls next door. She and Janet Powell didn't even know them well, as they hadn't been living there long. The only way they would even have come up in conversation, she maintains, is if she or Janet had mentioned how unusual it was at the time for two sets of single women to be sharing two houses, side by side. 'In those days, we might have laughed about how unusual it was, four single women living side by side like that. But that would have been the only way we'd have even talked about them.'

As Ilona again recalls the evening she, John Grant and her housemate stayed up talking into the early hours of the next morning, she becomes uncharacteristically disturbed about what detectives did and didn't ask her after she found their bodies three days later. 'I told them John was there with us and that he stayed the night on the couch,' she says. 'But they never asked me about how he came to be at the house, they never asked me about our "relationship", about how he acted that night, or whether I saw anybody hanging about outside, and no one's come back to me since.

No one's asked me any of these questions. Apart from my initial statement, I've never been spoken to again.'

Realising who could have been watching both houses from the street as the night wore on, Ilona is increasingly angry about what's been missed in the investigation. It dawns on her, too, what could have happened to her and Janet. 'Maybe John saved us by being there! Maybe Power did follow us home from the Celtic Club and somehow got the two houses mixed up. Or maybe he noticed Suzanne in the front room next door and decided to go in there instead?

'No one's come back to me about anything like this, let alone "are you sure John was on the couch all night?" All these things they should have asked, they didn't and still haven't. You'd have assumed that with a case of this magnitude, they'd be following up on everything, especially if, you know, they thought John was their number-one suspect. But nothing. It was weird.'

Those who knew John Joseph Power insist that he was capable of extreme violence – fuelled by a different aggression than his fighting mate Tommy Collins – and speculate that he had 'the form' to kill one, if not three, young women in the space of three years. Among the last people seen with a missing nineteen-year-old, and found guilty of raping another woman of the same age fifteen years later, Power could have been the one to wait, knock on the door when the suburb was quiet and overpower the two friends.

And John Grant truly would not have known a thing.

In time, detectives revealed that their initial list of suspects in the Easey Street case contained eight names. While they have never released these names publicly, four are obvious: the three men who had been inside the house and not seen the bodies, and John Grant.

A disgraced police officer, allegedly kicked off the force in the mid-1970s for sexually abusing women while on the job, also made this ominous register; so too a so-called 'champion sportsman', eventually identified as a racing-car driver, who purportedly knew Suzanne and had visited her at Easey Street, as well as a man detectives tracked all the way to Britain.

Perhaps most interesting was the possible eighth suspect on this rollcall, a man who lived in the Euroa/Benalla area and was known to both families. Early in the investigation, both Sue's brother Martin Bartlett and Suzanne's sister Gayle Armstrong had told police they suspected he could be involved.

He had gone out with Suzanne several years before she left Australia to travel overseas, was known to country police and had been in Melbourne at the time of the murders. A couple of days before the deaths, he and a friend had started drinking, 'and he was getting angry' at his home in northern Victoria, so his wife left for her parents as fast as she 'could get the kids in the car'.

By Monday, he was reportedly drinking at a pub in Collingwood, just blocks from Easey Street. He was said to be visiting his 'mistress' at the time, who provided him with an alibi, telling detectives he was with her in Fitzroy all night.

His wife claimed police interviewed him several times over the intervening decades. But never when she was present. 'They never came to the house, they always came to see him at work,' she recalled.

When we spoke in 2017, she was long separated from this man and fighting terminal illness. She wasn't sure he could have done 'something so violent' as commit murder, but alleged he had beaten her up before, and so believed she knew 'what he was capable of' when drunk. She seemed to take solace from the fact that he had told her a DNA test had cleared him, as it had the seven others on Homicide's 'list of eight'.

While the investigation seemed to be offering up many suspects, there was no apparent chief suspect to present in court. Maybe the official inquest would crack things open?

There can be few more daunting roles than that of a coroner, especially a senior coroner in a major jurisdiction. Not many have the spiritual strength to take the job on for any length of time. Fewer still have had the presence of Harry William Pascoe, Melbourne's chief coroner for two decades.

For lawyers, journalists and probably detectives too, the old Coroner's Court – perched on the edge of the city at the far end of Flinders Street, not quite South Melbourne, not quite the CBD – always felt an unfortunate place to be, certainly more sombre than other magistrates' courts around town. As senior journalist Geoffrey Barker described it, decades after being assigned there, it was 'where matters of life and death, public reputation and lethal crime were presided over by the bespectacled coroner … and where sadistic coppers in the morgue behind the court delighted in showing virgin reporters their chilled clientele stretched out naked on gurneys with labels tied to their toes'. So quiet was this courtroom that young journalists and staff alike would wince when they heard a loud noise coming from the annexe off to the side of the main room, as this often meant that another body was being delivered to the morgue.

This was Harry Pascoe's domain, his professional home for twenty-one years, and he cut a grave figure most mornings looking down from his magistrate's bench, pen and gavel never far from hand. Yet that was as it should be; there was little room for levity in this grief-filled arena. How could there be, as this 'special magistrate' inquired into how and sometimes why a person had died in abnormal circumstances, and who, if anyone, was responsible for their death?

Between 1958 and 1979, Pascoe investigated some of Victoria's more infamous deaths: the mysterious 'brain bleed' of Lady Anne Rylah, one of Australia's first female veterinarians and wife of then deputy premier Sir Arthur Rylah; Australian cricketer Jack Iverson's gunshot suicide; the thirty-five workers killed in the Westgate Bridge collapse; and the heart-rending case of six-month-old Margaret Loomes, suffocated with a plastic bag, and her two-year-old sister, thought at the time to be guilty of the murder (in fact, it was the girls' mother).

More straightforward but no less confronting, Harry Pascoe also signed off on the inquisition into the hanging of Ronald Ryan, the last person to be legally executed in Australia, in 1967.

Perhaps it was fitting then that, two years before stepping down from this demanding role, it was this particular coroner who took on the inquest into the Easey Street murders, which was held on 12 July 1977. The women's deaths deserved his attention. The case deserved this initial day in court.

By contemporary standards, the police brief the coroner was

presented with was alarmingly thin – basically a list of nine 'depositions of witnesses' and a box of twenty-seven exhibits. But according to those involved in such hearings at the time, this was probably a fuller folder than usual.

What's left on file in Victoria's public records office is disconcerting in its lack of volume and order. When I first inspected it, at the State Coroner's headquarters in Kavanagh Street in Melbourne's Southbank, the collection of statements was in disarray, and it seemed as if no one had bothered to open the file for many, many years. The pages, now quite fragile, were out of order, suggesting that the last person who had rifled through it had taken no care with the file's contents. Still, the information contained on the tissue-thin pages is substantial.

On 12 July 1977, just a day short of the women's bodies being found six months earlier, the inquest began. But journalistic interest in the case had waned; only a couple of reporters were there to cover the matter. The city's senior crime writers would have known that little new was going to be revealed in the evidence put to the court – except perhaps when Detective Senior Sergeant Alfred Oldfield put on the record that the Homicide Squad had not had any success in finding the killer.

Key witnesses in the case, including Martin Bartlett and Ilona Stevens, did not attend – or at least don't remember doing so – but their statements given to police months earlier were presented to the coroner.

His official written finding was as dry and proper as it was unsurprising: Armstrong and Bartlett had both died from 'multiple stab wounds then and there feloniously unlawfully and maliciously inflicted by a person or person unknown to me, and I further find that such person or persons did murder the deceased'.

'In their summing up of their investigation, police described the case as a very brutal murder,' *The Herald* reported Harry Pascoe as saying. 'That description sums up everything I have to say about it.'

It was hardly enough. But only Suzanne's father had the will to try to shake things up, once the inquest into his daughter's murder was over. Outside the court, on the city's grey edge, he said he thought the state government should at least double the $20,000 reward it was offering for information leading to the arrest and conviction of the killer.

Bill Armstrong's frustration and pain was palpable that day. But his plea went unheeded for almost another year. The Victorian government boosted the reward to $50,000 in June 1978. It would take thirty-nine years for it to reach the level no doubt he believed it deserved from the start.

CHAPTER 12
THE MEDIUM

NEARLY A YEAR after the coroner's inquest, and eighteen months after the two women's bodies were found in Collingwood, police had still not made an arrest. Perhaps more troubling was the fact that they seemed to have no real leads in their hunt for the murderer.

While most Australians were cheerfully enjoying *Grease* and *Superman* in cinemas that year, and the Bee Gees strangled the Top 10 with 'Night Fever' and 'Stayin' Alive', 24-year-old Gayle Armstrong battled a rising sense of desperation.

Still relatively new to the role of mother to her own son, let alone to her slain sister's little boy, and without the psychological support or media advice that families of murder victims have access to now, she was navigating the consequences of her sister's death as best she could. She even agreed to a request to take part in a 'reading' with a psychic. And not just any psychic.

At the time, British-born Doris Stokes was an internationally popular spiritualist, a professional medium who could fairly be described, at fifty-nine, as a 'rock star', her success the 1970s equivalent of America's John Edwards today. Her appearances on

The Don Lane Show prompted heated debate as she made 'contact' with dead relatives of the night-time talk show's studio audience.

Stokes toured the country, making public appearances in entertainment venues in five capital cities that year. Her sessions in various small churches were even more confronting, as hundreds queued for hours, waiting to be touched by her 'healing hands' as she stood not far from the altar, stained-glass windows rising behind her.

She claimed to have helped UK police solve a couple of difficult murder cases and, given the air of wonder that swirled around her, it's not hard to see why it might have occurred to a journalist to ask her to try to 'see' what happened at Easey Street. Nothing else had worked in terms of solving the double homicide, the reporter must have thought. What was there to lose?

The Sunday Press arranged the meeting between the media-savvy psychic and the grieving sister.

While Gayle can't quite recall how this 'special session' was organised, it seems that she drove from her family's home in Euroa to meet Stokes in Melbourne, with *Sunday Press* journalist Stephen O'Baugh and a photographer on hand to record it.

As they both settled into big, boxy armchairs, the medium explained she could not promise to make contact with Suzanne Armstrong. 'If I can't do it, I won't give you a lot of hearts and flowers,' she told Gayle.

She did much more than that.

Within minutes, Stokes claimed to have 'summoned' Suzanne's spirit and, over the next two hours, proceeded to tell her sister not only how both women had died, but the names of the *two* men who killed them and the location of the murder weapon.

She also identified the make of the murderers' car, explained how they had escaped from the house without being seen and outlined where she believed they were living. More disturbingly, this 'seer' told Gayle that her sister had known both men before they came to her house that night.

According to Stokes, the men entered through a kitchen window, and one went up the passage to Suzanne's bedroom, where he stood over her in bed. She said Suzanne 'told' her, 'I woke up and saw [name deleted] standing over me in my bed. There was something around my neck.'

Later in the session, she claimed she was being 'told' the weapon was 'a tradesman's tool, possibly a chisel, something used to slice wood'. O'Baugh's story in *The Sunday Press* continued,

> At this stage, Gayle wept as Mrs Stokes, on behalf of Suzanne, said 'why … why, why' and kept repeating the name of her killer. 'He's the swine,' Mrs Stokes cried in a burst of emotion.
>
> Interpreting the getaway, Mrs Stokes said the killers rolled up their blood-soaked clothes and rushed to a vehicle they had left in a nearby dead-end street. They then drove off to the country about 50 kilometres from Melbourne. Mrs Stokes said: 'They drove up a steep hill, up quite high and with a drop into a valley.'
>
> When asked to name the area, Mrs Stokes took a map. With her eyes half closed, she traced a finger along the Hume Highway and suddenly clutched her heart. She said: 'I feel a pain here.'
>
> Her finger was resting on the Pretty Sally area. 'That's where they dropped the evidence,' she claimed.

Forty years later, the article makes disturbing reading, and fails to capture how challenging this session must have been for Gayle. Coping with the intensity of Doris Stokes' performance was one thing, but dealing with the specific details she was 'receiving' was an entirely different matter – especially without any professional support or an advocate to help her through the meeting and debrief after it was over. Like so much that has occurred in and around this murder case over the decades, such an encounter would probably not be allowed to proceed in this manner now.

But the still-grieving sister remembers it as an overwhelmingly positive experience. 'It was an experience. She [Stokes] just sticks in my brain,' Gayle says firmly. 'I don't remember the two names, no – but no, no, it was amazing. She was so nice.'

Gayle insists that her memory isn't good, which is why she can't remember the two names Stokes 'conjured' during their meeting. 'I can't tell you, I don't know, I'm hopeless; my brain ... it just doesn't [get there] ... and it's not funny, I can tell you.' But the British medium left an impression. 'It was out of this world, *she* was out of this world. But don't ask me any questions, because I can't remember.'

There is one thing that does stick in her mind about their meeting. She was especially moved when, near the end of their time together, the clairvoyant mentioned that Gayle was wearing something of her sister's, a cardigan she still has to this day. 'She knew exactly what I had on of Suzanne's. Doris was definitely an eerie person. She knew something. She's a smart lady, I remember *that*.'

According to the *Sunday Press* reporter, Gayle was 'ashen-faced' as her meeting with Stokes ended. She described some of the things the medium had raised as 'startling' and said she would 'beg' police to follow up the new claims. She also vowed to take a tape recording of the meeting to police, so they could hear what she had heard.

In response to the article, the head of the Homicide Squad was blunt with the media. Detective Chief Inspector Paul Delianis made clear that his officers were 'concerned with the natural, not the supernatural'. He also denied the strange report the newspaper had run two days earlier, indicating that police were going to take part in the 'séance' with the psychic and Gayle. 'None of my detectives has been to any such performance by Mrs Stokes. I am concerned that the squad has been involved in a showmanship atmosphere, or is seen to be promoting her act,' Delianis said. 'I am not making any comment publicly on her ability or inability to make contact with the spirits. But that's not the way we conduct our investigations, and my men didn't go anywhere near her.' He added that the 'clairaudient' should contact police if she had evidence about unsolved murders. 'If they bring a tape in, we'll listen to it. But we're concerned only with tangible evidence.'

Gayle didn't have a copy of either the reporter's tape recording or notes of her session with Stokes. So nothing came of the 'information' Stokes revealed. She says the police dismissed the more serious details about the murders that the medium provided, and which were published in the *Sunday Press* article, such as the location of the murder weapon. She recalls their response was along the lines of 'oh, she's just silly': 'She said that the knife or the weapon – something's buried on Pretty Sally and could pinpoint it to a certain spot. But the police weren't interested. Pretty Sally is the big hill before you're going down into Wallan, just after Kilmore, but they didn't go and see it ... That just went dead, because I was in no position to be going digging anywhere.' She allows herself a quick laugh. 'So it all fell by the wayside.'

Soon after her session with Gayle, Doris Stokes made another public link regarding the Easey Street murders. In Melbourne to appear on *The Don Lane Show* on GTV9, Mrs Stokes spoke to actress Lorraine Bayly, star of the long-running serial *The Sullivans*, which Sue and Suzanne had watched the night they were killed.

'I had contact with Lorraine's father, Eric, on the other side,' Mrs Stokes told journalist Tom Prior. 'All of a sudden I started reeling off names and streets. I had never heard of the streets before. I mentioned names and I mentioned a psychiatric hospital, so we got out some maps and started going over them.' Prior noted that Stokes, who 'spoke in a pronounced London accent', said she was 'controlled completely by spirits "on the other side" when speaking of Easey Street. "I am only the medium," she said, adding, to ally doubts, "I'm like your mum, lovey. She wouldn't take you down, would she?"'

It's not hard to understand why the visiting clairvoyant so infuriated detectives at the time. Yet, nearly thirty years later, the Armstrong family would again be told that a psychiatric facility was pivotal to solving the case. But this time, the information would come from a more mundane source: a former patient.

A quarter of a century after the Doris Stokes 'intervention', the Armstrong family had a second brush with the paranormal. A television production company approached Gayle to take part in an episode of *Sensing Murder*. Based on the Swedish prototype, the series paired up psychics and private investigators to examine unsolved murders.

Back in the little house in Easey Street, the Australian team wandered through the rented, unrenovated property, 'sensing' different moods in different rooms as they recounted what had occurred on the night of 10 January 1977. 'Yeah, those girls went into the house and told the reporter what they felt as they went,' Gayle recalls. She did not go with them. 'No way.'

Nothing useful came from this visit, in terms of new clues or information. Police refused to have anything to do with the makers of the program. The series was eventually canned, and although it was revived in 2017 its track record in solving cold cases is poor.

Debbie Malone, a Sydney-based medium who worked on four episodes in the first run of *Sensing Murder*, says the program 'was really disappointing. They got police off-side and one of the original psychics declined to keep going with the show because of death threats she received.'

Malone claims to have worked 'with the assistance of police' on high-profile cases including the backpacker murders in Belangalo State Forest in New South Wales and the Claremont murders in Perth. She says that in her experience, Australian police will not admit publicly that they work with 'mediums, psychics and the like', but some do. She suspects that, despite extraordinary advances in forensic science, the general attitude towards psychic and spiritual inquiry has not evolved since the late 1970s, at least not within the police force. 'The community has a broader appreciation of what we do. But I think the police worry that this kind of work shows them up in some way, that it gives people the idea that they don't really know what they're doing. I believe we can complement each other's work.'

During the filming of the episode, Gayle was more taken with one of the psychics in the group who focused on her personally, predicting that she was going to be moving around quite a bit. 'She told me I was going to travel ... I was going to do a lot of travel. And I thought, *far out, lady – you couldn't have been more right*. Ten years I've been travelling,' she says with a laugh. A woman always on the move.

CHAPTER 13

THE BOOK

As the decades passed, the deaths of Susan Armstrong and Sue Bartlett were never far from the minds of the detectives who first walked into their home on 13 January 1977, or for those in the local community in and around Collingwood. But Doris Stokes' grandiose performance was the last time the Easey Street murders made the front page of a newspaper or led a radio or television news bulletin in Australia. 'Milestone' dates – five years, ten, then fifteen since the women's deaths – slipped by relatively unnoticed, given there was little more for the media to do than recap well-worn details.

It wasn't until the year before the twentieth 'anniversary' of the double homicide that a senior crime reporter took it up again.

Tom Prior had been a journalist with Melbourne's *Sun* newspaper for twenty-eight years, twenty of them as a crime reporter, and had worked at *Truth* before that.

'Like some of the police involved,' he wrote, 'I developed an anger, a hatred and contempt for the killer.' He also believed 'the Easey Street murder investigation was handicapped from the start' because some influential police started it with pre-conceived ideas.

They blamed the victims. 'Crime reporters, "in the pockets" of police as some were at one stage or another, went along with the charade and a monster got away with a shocking crime,' he wrote.

He began to reinvestigate the case, speaking to friends and family of the women, and eventually wrote a book about it.

Prior was undergoing chemotherapy for cancer as his work, *They Trusted Men*, took shape. Published in 1996, the book attracted attention but unfortunately, as driven as he was to solve the double homicide, the ex-boxer ended up reducing the women to stereotypes. This might have been due to the pace at which he was working, as a result of ill health. But he also seemed to struggle with his own sense of what independent women could and couldn't do without coming to grief. His perspective seemed at odds with that of the changing era.

In his book, Prior often refers to how the two women looked and how many boyfriends they had; early on, describing how Suzanne moved through various jobs after she left school, he wrote: 'As soon as she was promoted, it seemed to her puzzled mother, she moved on – with David, Greg, Max, Rob ...' This list went on. Later, he quoted a male friend as saying Sue was 'a large, pleasant woman – did you know that they were known as "Big Sue" and "Little Sue" ... it started when they were at school in Benalla.'

For all the good journalistic 'digging' he did, the book was also confusing: beyond the immediate Armstrong and Bartlett families, the names of all the people involved in the case, most of whom Tom Prior interviewed, were changed for legal reasons. It didn't help that the pseudonyms he chose sounded like characters in daytime soap operas.

To research the case, Prior and Owen McKenna, the colleague who worked with him on the project, were granted unprecedented access to the case files at police headquarters. At the time, this wasn't surprising. Both men were veteran crime reporters and so known to the Homicide Squad. Like Prior, McKenna had worked at *Truth*. 'Owen was a drinker, a gambler, a hard-worker, a no-nonsense reporter ... [we] disagreed about many things – but agreed on the important ones ... the [Easey Street] investigation could have been handled better by some police and most of the news media.'

Suzanne Armstrong's mother and a good friend also allowed him to quote from several deeply personal letters that Suzanne had written, some from when she was travelling, before settling in Naxos, leading up to the birth of her son. Gayle Armstrong permitted him to use some correspondence she and her sister had shared. She regrets having done so now.

Prior also tracked down the father of Suzanne's child, Manolis Margaritis, in Greece, and helped him connect with Greg Armstrong in Melbourne. To this day, he remains the only journalist Greg has spoken to at length. 'The worst thing is not to know who did it,' Suzanne's son told the veteran crime reporter two decades ago. 'There is nothing I can do, but it would be different if I knew. For one thing, it would be something big I wouldn't have to think about every day. The best thing about my father is he's a top bloke, but it would be good even if he wasn't, if he was ordinary. From all accounts, the last thing my mother could be described as was "ordinary". I miss her. I wish I could meet my mother again, even just once.'

The poignancy of Greg's remark was immediately overshadowed by the author's next sentence: 'Too many men had experience of Suzanne Armstrong, but few had anything to say against her.'

Despite his censorious descriptions of both women's sexual activity throughout the book, Tom Prior was a determined and diligent reporter as he dug back into the case, looking at as many angles as he could, physically as well as intellectually. He even made an appointment to inspect 147 Easey Street – where he reached a surprising conclusion.

In 1995, the little Victorian terrace was pretty much as it had been in 1977, but the adjoining house next door, where Ilona Stevens and Janet Powell had lived, had been knocked down. Intriguingly, Prior came away thinking that it would have been hard for Ilona and Janet – and their overnight guest, John Grant – to have heard what was going on next door, even though they shared a common wall. 'Standing in a parking area, which was the site of 149, I could hardly hear a thing when [they] turned up the volume as loud as it could go in 147,' he wrote. 'The thin brick wall of the old building was near perfect insulation; most of the sound which could be heard coming from the backyard of the house, not through the wall.'

For good measure, he also noted that 'light definitely came through the glass above the front door into the passage however, and I found it hard to understand how Ridge and Hamilton [pseudonyms] could have failed to see Bartlett's body. Ridge said he didn't look, and Hamilton said he was drunk. Both then were lucky.'

Legally constrained as he was, Prior alluded to who he believed was the killer, but only after stating that he thought no one would be charged with the crime. 'No, I do not think the Easey Street murders will ever be solved, certainly not to a jury's satisfaction,' he wrote.

> Barring confessions – and if there was to be a serious one, surely it would have been heard before now – there is little chance of charges being laid. If there were an accessory, he or she was very much after the event and the event, the murders, [was] committed by a man.
>
> Semen was found in the blood under Suzanne Armstrong's body ... but someone stabbed the "two Sues" 84 [sic] times; who was it? The longer I investigated the murders, studied the transcripts of my interviews and at least early on, POLICE records – the more I honed in on one man. Twenty years later, I am at least three-quarters convinced, he did it!

This 'person of interest' knew Suzanne, he maintained, and her father had even expressed 'strong suspicions about him' before he died. But Prior alleged this man was 'not really investigated because he was "trusted" as a former associate of some police':

> He had an association with Suzanne Armstrong, but claimed he spurned her. He had been to 147 Easey Street and knew the location of the various rooms. He had a violent temper. His marriage had broken down, and a number of previous sexual associations had failed ... He had assaulted women before. He was known to be drinking at the time of the murders, but had not drunk alcohol for a long time after them. He had given

contradictory accounts of his movements during the murder week. And he was not robustly investigated.

What Tom Prior does not reveal in this second-last chapter is that he had interviewed the man he put forward as 'worth another look' and come away from the encounter quite shaken.

Prior went as close as he could in *They Trusted Men* to revealing this man's identity, but the title of 'labourer' didn't tell the whole story. His main suspect was a former police officer kicked off the force a couple of years before the murders after sexually harassing women he stopped for traffic infringements. He was known to have worked on at least one of the active construction sites close to Easey Street around the time of the killings, and some police believe he had met Suzanne Armstrong. They also considered him a possible suspect.

Publisher Michael Wilkinson recalls the ailing journalist meeting his 'prime suspect' towards the end of the project. He says Prior told him he played this person of interest a tape recording that took him by surprise, and it elicited quite an aggressive response. 'Tom met that cop and played him a tape,' Wilkinson says. 'I'm not sure what was on it, I don't know. But when asked about killing the girls, the cop told him, "Not saying I did or I didn't, but you can't prove anything."'

'Tom seemed to be very rattled by the meeting. Very,' the publisher recalls. 'But he was also quite addled himself at the end of doing that book, due to the chemotherapy he was undergoing. It really knocked him around.'

Two years after *They Trusted Men* was published, DNA testing started being used in Australia. Eventually, the disgraced officer was cleared of involvement in the double homicide.

Following Tom Prior's death, Andrew Rule, one of Australia's best journalists working the crime beat, lauded 'the old sleuth's' bravery in pursuing the case. 'What Prior didn't write, but later told this writer,' Rule revealed, 'was that while he was researching his book, a man telephoned his house at 2 am one morning and threatened his wife. The caller warned that Prior should "stop asking questions" and ended the conversation with "I know where you live."' Rule reported that Prior thought someone in the force must have tipped off the former cop that he was asking about him. 'He said he hoped nothing like that would interfere with the integrity of blood samples for DNA tests, which apparently cleared the former policeman along with the other seven suspects tested in 1998.'

Tom Prior's book foreshadowed an awakening public fascination in cold cases, as well as tapping in to the very specific interest in the Easey Street tragedy. Perhaps more significantly, his investigation led to Greg Armstrong reuniting with his father.

But however unintentionally, it also tarnished the reputations of his mother and her best friend. Battling serious illness and racing to finish his work, it was as if he couldn't quite grasp the character, let alone the vibrancy, of the two women whose murderer he was so intent on finding.

CHAPTER 14

THE LETTERS

'I THINK THAT, afterwards, the monster was genuinely shocked by what he had done and tried to reform. But there are some things so bad they simply cannot be forgiven or forgotten,' Tom Prior wrote in *They Trusted Men*.

But who was this monster? Despite so many theories about who the killer may have been, police were no closer to making an arrest.

As the years passed, the original team of detectives moved on to other cases. New information about what had happened on that January night in 1977 was just not forthcoming from the public. Many following this case closely came to believe that the police had been too dogged in their pursuit of just one 'person of interest' – journalist John Grant – and now he and the other seven names on the original list of suspects had been cleared by DNA testing, they were forced to wait for new information to come to light in order to progress the investigation. The truth was as hard to accept as it was to comprehend: the high-profile double homicide that Peter Hiscock and his colleagues had been so sure would be easy to solve was becoming one of the Homicide Squad's most perplexing cases.

Over the decades, too, it turned into a public relations dilemma for the Victorian police force. How often could they make appeals for information without the community asking why there were no serious developments in this notorious case? How much time and resources should be devoted to such an old murder?

Then came the letters.

The first of the six arrived, without fanfare, at the start of 2004.

Written in the old-fashioned script of a student schooled in the 1940s, full of loops and flourishes, it was dated 30 January and addressed to Bruce Currie, Suzanne Armstrong's stepfather.

The first two sentences were startling. 'Dear Bruce,' it read. 'It's terribly sad that your wife and the two families were cheated because of the criminal negligence of Larundel Hospital. Then to add insult to injury, the Homicide Squad have known for four years and five months … that Anthony Thomas Christie could be the Easey Street killer (which he is) but chose pathetic sad games instead of a proper investigation.'

The letter came from a man named Peter Collier. Without revealing anything specific about his own mental health, he said he had been a patient at Larundel Psychiatric Hospital in Melbourne in the early months of 1977, when his friend 'Jack' Christie was admitted 'in a coma' after attempting suicide towards the end of January 1977.

In this first letter, which apparently followed a phone call to Currie, Collier outlined Christie's background: the son of an SP bookie who died when he was young, he claimed he did 'time' in the old Turana Boys Home (now Youth Detention Centre) before getting married and divorced and having a son of his own. But he was a 'top crim', according to Collier, and a physically dominating man.

Over the next seven months, Peter Collier tried to convince Eileen and Bruce Currie of what he fervently believed: that his friend had murdered the two young women in Collingwood and then, a couple of weeks later, tried to kill himself because of the 'terrible act he had committed'.

Throughout his next five letters, his handwriting growing increasingly erratic and his thoughts circuitous, Collier returned to this key allegation: Christie had been admitted to Larundel in a coma that lasted ten days, and three weeks after regaining consciousness told two different group therapy sessions that he liked to 'carve up' women after having sex with them.

'Christie said in group therapy that after having sex with a woman (any woman) he felt like getting a carving knife and killing them: you can see what he was about,' he said, in his second dispatch.

> Christie didn't know if the staff were "cat-mousing" him; he had to find out whether or not he'd said something incriminating about the murders, this was his way of finding out.
>
> It was only a small group of seven or eight patients, or clients as they are now known. The therapist should have discussed what he said with the rest of the staff; the statement was bizarre, because women liked Christie and Christie liked women. He said once 'I've had my share,' a real understatement.
>
> About a week later, Christie repeated the statement in group therapy, again making sure that he hadn't said something

> incriminating coming out of the coma ... it would have been about this time of the year 27 years ago.

This letter was dated 11 February 2004.

Collier did not say much about himself in this determined yet ragged correspondence, although he made clear he was in New South Wales in the early part of January 1977, before being admitted to Larundel, one of Victoria's old 'mental asylums'.

It probably wasn't surprising that he tried to keep his background to himself. Larundel had been closed for several years by the time he contacted the Curries, but it had an infamous reputation, and it is clear he assumed they would have known of the facility when he told them about his time in North 5 Ward.

Opened in 1953, the hospital catered for those struggling with severe psychiatric illness. The initial intake of 387 patients expanded to 750 within two years, including 270 women. Peter Dupas, one of Victoria's most heinous serial killers, spent two weeks as an in-patient there in 1968, when he was just fifteen. By the time its doors closed in 1999 to make way for community-based care, the institution was seen as a relic of a draconian era. The site is currently undergoing a $500 million renovation, with contemporary-style apartments being built to adjoin the original red-brick Building 1.

While Collier didn't provide information about his time inside the facility, or even the length of his stay, he did share a curious detail at the end of some of his letters. After his signature, he often wrote the number sequence 28-12-31. Was this his birth date and, in his mind, a way of convincing the family that he was trying to right a wrong before he died, before it really was too late?

He certainly tried every tack to persuade them of his theory. By his third letter, written on 23 February 2004, he quickly came to the point, outlining what he believed happened at 147 Easey Street. The spelling mistakes are Colliers' own.

> This is only guesswork, but I knew Christie and it's the only thing that makes any sense to me.
>
> I don't believe for a moment that Suzanne was raped, it's possible but highly improbable: if your capable of butchering two women, your capable of making out that one of them was raped.
>
> A far more likely scenario is that Suzanne and Christie were involved: in 'pillow talk', he's told her Suzanne that he's killed a couple of crims (he'd hinted at that to me). The women have decided to get rid of Christie and they have threatened him with the police. He's lost control, their dead ...
>
> Consider this; Christie was thirty years old, probably nearing the height of his power as a tough, clever, resourceful crim and yet he destroys two women, nearly destroys himself; Why? For me, there is only one logical answer, he lost control; what would have made him lose control: his hatred for the Police.
>
> I've raised some questions that can never be answered until we stand before the Lord at Judgement Day. I'm terribly sorry for any extra pain that I have caused you, but I've mixed with dangerous people, I know what they are capable of. Believe me, I'm sorry for your pain.

The unusual correspondent sent Eileen and Bruce Currie a fourth note in March 2004 to say that he was leaving his home in Bright, but offering to meet them before he left. They didn't take up that suggestion, although they politely wrote back to him to decline. He wrote again, a month later.

> Thank you for your letter, it was very gracious of you ... I will carry some guilt to the grave that Christies wasn't apprehended twenty seven years ago. When [he] made his statement in Group Therapy at Larundel, it was on the tip of my tongue to say 'have you ever killed somebody Jack?'. The reason I didn't speak up was that I wasn't in good shape myself, however it was at that moment I knew he was a killer, sadly I had no idea who he had killed.
>
> My failure however certainly doesn't excuse the staff at Larundel who were criminally negligent in not working out that Christie was the Easey Street killer.

Throughout this correspondence, Peter Collier was obsessed with what he believed to be the authorities' failure to properly comprehend the information to which they were privy – specifically, Jack Christie's confessions in therapy that he liked 'carving up women' after having sex with them. In his mind, Larundel staff should have alerted detectives about what was said in the two group therapy sessions he cites.

A couple of months went by before he wrote to Bruce and Eileen Currie one more time. In this letter written in July 2004, he revealed – if unwittingly – an emotional volatility that underscored his relentless focus on the case. 'You may not like the tone of this letter, but I'm tired of pussy-footing around,' he wrote. 'I'm an old man and could die any time. I'm surprised, no amazed really, that Greg didn't want to see me. Sure, it would have been distressing to see a close friend of his mother's killer, but so what? You can drown in self-pity you know.'

'While I'm alive you've got a chance to get the truth out in the public domain,' he continued.

> You stand to gain by it as I have told you ... I put it in writing to Homicide that I wouldn't touch a cent of the $50,000 reward, it should go to the relatives of the victims ... There is one way to get the truth out and that is to put it out on the Internet that Anthony Thomas Christie is the Easey Street killer and the evidence proving it. That would put some pressure on the creeps covering up the truth.

This was the last letter Collier sent the Curries for three years. No one knows why he stopped at that point in 2004, or why, on 10 January 2007 he sent them what turned out to be his final missive. Obviously, the date of his writing, exactly thirty years on from the murders, was not a coincidence. It's clear, too, that the family hadn't been far from his thoughts. Nor have they forgotten him; he said he had actually been to visit Suzanne's youngest sister, Loretta.

> Your probably aware that I was at Loretta's place last Friday night. I told her that I was too old to go back to the ranges at Bright but I'm heading back there: I'm staying at the Star pub at the moment.

> Last Monday, I went to the Police Complex at 412 St Kilda Rd and saw Det. Sgt Stuart Bateson and surprise, surprise! I liked him. We went over the case again. I told him that Christie had a son, and although I never met him I had seen his photo and there was no doubt who his father was … he [Christie's son] was a street fighter, had worked out with [the] Supreme Court to get Christie exhumed …
>
> I told Bateson that Christie had told me that his son hated him so that could make it easier to get DNA from him. Bateson said he would keep an open mind on the subject with regards to deciding whether or not to approach Christie's son.
>
> Bateson also said that I must stop sending him abusive cards, I said fair enough … [he] shook hands a couple of times and treated me decently; he's not a standover type but at times you can see that steel in him.

Gayle Armstrong says that when Peter Collier first contacted her mother and Bruce, they met with him to discuss his allegations and try to ascertain why he had chosen to reveal this information 'out of the blue'. She also remembers how convincing some of what he put forward in the largely one-way correspondence seemed. 'You read it as if it is really true,' she muses. 'And why would someone make all this up? He wrote like he did know [something].'

For some reason that he never explained, Collier had mentioned Terry Armstrong in one of his letters, writing: 'Which begs the question, did Terence know that Christie was involved with his sister and was too scared to tell the police? Christie had charm, but he was bad news, dangerous and in those days his crim mates would have been scary as well. A crim at Pentridge said Jack Christie has got a name for getting things done.'

Gayle has no idea why he brought her brother into the equation. 'Maybe he had done his homework on us [but] he didn't know any of us.'

Any hope Eileen and Bruce had that Peter Collier could shed light on what had happened to Suzanne and her friend dissipated when they talked to detectives about his allegations. Despite Collier's repeated assertion about his friend Jack Christie being the Easey Street killer, police dismissed the scenario. 'They said he was a loony and had done it before to other people ... so who knows?' Gayle says. She recalls they were told that the 76-year-old was known to them before he started making this specific claim. 'So no, not really any good.' It must have been crushing that what appeared a promising new lead from a 'fresh source', the first in many years, and couched in such intimate detail, ended up going nowhere.

Even though Anthony 'Jack' Christie had died a decade before Collier wrote his letters, the family wanted to believe the information about Christie was real. They hoped that the monster they had chased through the shadows for so long could at last have a face. In the wake of this particular disappointment, they joined Support After Murder, a victims group that had been set up by a couple whose son had been stabbed to death.

At the time, co-founder Bruce Kimball said there was a need for a support group for 'those touched by the murder of a loved one'.

'We support each other, because we've been there too,' he said. 'When you talk to Eileen, it's like talking to all the other mothers whose children have been murdered; they share a similar pain. For Eileen, she needs closure by knowing who killed her daughter.'

It's not hard to imagine why Eileen pinned hope on the content of a stranger's letters. Much of what the former psych-hospital resident suggested seemed credible. The postal address he used throughout this correspondence – Bright Post Office, in north-eastern Victoria – is genuine.

And locals do remember him. According to one, who does not wish to be named, Collier 'lived in just a bark or a tin hut somewhere in the bush out there' and 'always seemed a little bit strange'. When he was in town, he would spend time in the pub as well as the post office, and 'he always talked about Bateson, Stuart Bateson'. 'Does that ring a bell?' the local asks.

It does, of course: Detective Bateson had worked on the cold case as a member of the Homicide Squad. He is now an assistant commissioner with Victoria Police. Collier never explained to his Bright acquaintance why he was mentioning the detective, or what it was about. 'Nope, he didn't tell me much more. But he was always talking about him.'

'He used to come in, and drift in and out,' this Bright local confides. 'He'd have to be in his eighties now, yeah, for sure, and the last time I saw him, he didn't look so good.' That was at least five years ago, this local says, and he doubts Collier is still alive.

The basic facts that Peter Collier sets out about his time at Larundel Psychiatric Hospital are harder to determine, almost lost in history's bureaucratic vault. The facility closed twenty-six years ago, and records listing admissions and discharges are no longer publicly accessible. But the psychiatrist Collier named, in his old-fashioned script, in that first letter to the Curries, did work at the old hospital. He was also director of clinical services at another hospital, part of Victoria's Office of Psychiatric Services.

Of course, it's unclear how much so senior a psychiatrist would have had to do with either Jack Christie or Peter Collier. Similarly, precisely why the men had been admitted to the facility, how long they stayed, and if they were treated on a long-term, outpatient basis after they returned to the community cannot be determined. But I understand that detectives never contacted the psychiatrist about any of his previous patients at Larundel.

Should doctors at Larundel have contacted police directly if these concerns about Christie came to their attention? Lester Walton, one of Victoria's most respected criminal psychologists, says his professional colleagues have an 'overriding duty' to report anyone they believe has committed a crime. 'You can be sued if you don't respond accurately,' he explains in the mid-city Melbourne office he has worked in for decades.

Given this double homicide was so prominently covered in the media at the time, staff would have been aware of the case. 'The fact that it was topical may well have been the reason it was in his delusions ... He's clearly become obsessed by it. But that's not to say it's untrue. It could be the opposite, in fact ... [We] can assume he was psychotic or very seriously depressed and so open to this story. So it could be his fantasy.'

Walton explains that Larundel was part of Victoria's 'psychopolis,' three psychiatric hospitals that admitted patients on a lower threshold than that required for admission today. Nevertheless, they had serious illnesses that couldn't be treated in the community.

But the likelihood, he thinks, 'of someone doing something like that and not being picked up' by DNA testing is 'minimal'. For this reason, Lester Walton is not convinced that a serial killer was involved in the Easey Street killings. 'But it's a very unusual crime. Most murders occur "in house" and are solved quickly.' In other words, most victims know their murderers.

Peter Collier has not contacted anyone attached to the case for more than a decade now. Nor has he gone public again – as he did once, in 2005, with rather mysterious flourish. If the '28-12-31' he included in his letters was indeed his birthdate, he would be eighty-seven now. If he is alive, perhaps this book will draw him out of hiding.

CHAPTER 15

THE HUNT

IN 2005, A YEAR after the Armstrong family started receiving Peter Collier's letters, I was working on *Background Briefing*, the ABC's weekly investigative documentary program on Radio National. I approached the Victorian Homicide Squad for an update on the Easey Street case. Was it 'open', being actively investigated? The answer was plain: not really. With DNA testing eliminating the main suspects from the Homicide Squad's original list, the investigation was stalled.

Greg Armstrong, Suzanne's then thirty-year-old son, declined to be interviewed for the show and did not mention Collier's letters. But during a short telephone conversation we had at the end of March 2005, he suggested I contact Stuart Bateson. He said the detective was the only police officer he knew who had been looking into the case.

I gained clearance to speak to Detective Bateson, who seemed to welcome a journalist taking interest in the case. In our short, introductory chat on the phone, he told me he kept this murder file close to hand. 'Information trickles in from time to time and we look at it,' he said. 'We're lucky in this case because we have a DNA sample of the offender.' He seemed quietly frustrated at the lack of progress made in recent years, despite the many new forensic techniques available to the Homicide team. Perhaps because of this, he seemed willing to discuss the matter – as long as I had permission to do so from his superiors. We scheduled an interview for the following week.

But an hour before we were due to meet at police headquarters in St Kilda Road, Stuart Bateson rang to say that permission had been withdrawn. No reason was given.

Fourteen years later, nothing has changed. In the course of working on this book, I have not been granted permission to speak with any detectives from the cold case squad about the Easey Street murders, despite making repeated official requests (and unofficial appeals) over the past two years.

'I think for a story not to be resolved leaves us with this anxiety. This is why we need to hear these stories again and again,' Helen Garner reflected, as part of the radio documentary Detective Bateson could not take part in. 'To see them resolved, even in fantasy … somehow releases that anxiety for us momentarily. It doesn't take it away forever, unfortunately, and that's why stories of murder will always be popular.' She illuminated why we as a community are so troubled by unsolved cases: 'We always want to hear the story again, we want to hear about the crime, we want to hear about the investigation, we want to hear about the person being found, charged, convicted and punished. We need to have that whole sequence replayed over and over. And when it can't be, when there's a "cold case", I think our anxiety rushes to that case, and kind of clusters around it in a desperate need for resolution.'

Despite the lack of new leads in the Easey Street case, it hadn't stopped police from looking for them, and attempting to gain some small sense of resolution for the Armstrong and Bartlett families. In 1998, two Melbourne detectives, Steve Tragardh and Rod Collins, flew to the United Kingdom and, working with colleagues from Scotland Yard, tracked down an Australian living in Margate, 'a shabby holiday town on the Kent coast smelling of fish and chip fat and poverty'. Journalist Andrew Rule reported the events vividly in his 2017 book *Rule on Crime*:

> They didn't know their quarry's exact address, but computer checks showed that he had been collecting his dole money from this particular office. It was pay day. He was a certainty to turn up.
>
> Sure enough, the man collected his dole and the detectives collected him ... they took him to the local police station, the Yard men saying all they needed was a tiny blood sample – a routine precaution, they said soothingly, which would eliminate him from a local inquiry.
>
> The suspect gave it willingly, so willingly that Tragardh and Collins wondered right then if it was a wild goose chase. Tragardh pocketed the vial of blood and they returned to London to extradite another murder suspect, which was the official reason for their flying visit.
>
> The detective kept the blood sample safely in his possession until he handed it over to the staff at Victoria police forensic science centre back in Melbourne. Days later, a forensic expert compared the DNA code in the English blood

> sample with DNA taken from what was coyly called a 'body fluid' taken from the crime scene almost exactly 22 years before ... It was negative.

While this foray proved unsuccessful, another international trip had a more promising outcome for the Easey Street case, and others like it. Ron Iddles, who in 1977 was a young uniformed police officer working at Collingwood CIB, found the perfect training ground in those hardscrabble streets for his future as a Homicide detective. 'I remember being called to three or four suicides where people had jumped off the high-rise buildings at 229 and 253 Hoddle Street. At 241 Wellington Street too,' he is quoted as saying in Justine Ford's biography of him, *The Good Cop*. 'I remember one call in which a male had jumped from the eighteenth floor. By the time we arrived someone had put a blanket over him, but you could see a lot of blood and skull parts. Was I horrified? At times those things can affect you, but back then it didn't really worry me. It was part of the job.'

There were times, too, when police did welfare checks on people no one had seen for weeks and they were discovered decomposing in their own home: 'The smell was horrible.'

The Painters and Dockers Union members were also Collingwood regulars, moving from the docks to their favourite hotels around the suburb. As a detective, Ron Iddles worked in major divisions including Homicide and the National Crime Authority before retiring to start his own trucking business in 1993. He returned to the force a few years later as a constable, and worked his way back into Homicide as a detective. In 1999, he was awarded the Angela

Taylor Memorial Scholarship, set up in memory of Constable Angela Rose Taylor after she died in the Russell Street car bombing in 1986, and he travelled to the United States to study how the FBI and police across North America investigated unsolved murders.

He was particularly impressed with the new teams in place in major police departments that dealt with cold cases – murders and other serious crimes where the trail had gone cold years, sometimes decades, earlier. Rather than packing away these old files, out of sight, leaving them to gather dust somewhere until new information came in and someone in Homicide had time to work it, cases were being treated in a new way – police were seeing the value in employing 'fresh eyes', specifically searching for ways to unravel some of the most troubling unsolved crimes.

When Iddles returned to Melbourne, he persuaded the powers that be at Victoria Police to follow this new model, and the state's first cold case unit was set up, with Detective Sergeant Ron Iddles as its chief.

He was only allocated three detectives to work with him, and it came as no surprise when the unit disappeared in a department reshuffle a couple of years later.

But another internal revamp saw it re-established in 2011. Iddles says early after the unit was re-established, he worked out which of Victoria's 280 unsolved homicides since 1950 were worth the team's attention. He went through the unsolved 'jobs' on the books and colour-coded them all – red indicating cases that were 'probably never going to be solved', yellow for the ones that 'needed a total overhaul' and green for those they could 'probably solve'. The Easey Street case was colour-coded green, 'due to the fact that there was DNA'.

Several months later, the cold case unit announced they had identified thirty unsolved homicides that they described as 'highly solvable'. In fact, Iddles explained that his team – by now four detectives and a sergeant – had set themselves a target: to review twenty-five unsolved murders a year.

'I think it is important ... the community actually has faith that we never give up,' he said. 'Detectives look at what witnesses are still available; whether DNA exists or could be obtained; if all the exhibits still exist; whether relationships between people who provided alibis for suspects have changed to such an extent they might want to retract the alibi and whether any new evidence or intelligence has come in since the original investigation. The more of those boxes that are ticked, the higher priority the case becomes.'

Eventually the team morphed into the current cold case squad. With sixteen dedicated detectives, as many as the entire Homicide team had in 1977, it's well resourced. 'Today, Force Command has a very strong commitment to investigating cold-case homicides,' Iddles told the media, before his retirement from Victoria Police in 2017. 'The way it is structured within Homicide now ... is fantastic. The cold case detectives are doing a great job. They have more resources than ever, are looking at more investigations than were ever done in the past and they are getting great results.'

He should know. After twenty-five years spent investigating some 300 murders, much has been made of Ron Iddles' conviction rate, which is around the 95 per cent mark. But that niggling 5 per cent worries him, and the Easey Street case is close to the top of that list. In his 'second coming' at Homicide, he oversaw two fresh inquiries into Suzanne Armstrong and Sue Bartlett's murders and was actively involved in trying to solve the case right up until he handed in his detective's badge.

Despite his oft-stated belief that 'the answer's in the file', a mantra family members have heard many times over many years, Iddles could not find the answer in this one.

Significantly, he blames the early work done in the case for this. 'I think they had too many "persons of interest"... [and] maybe a lack of forensic methods back then; they had blood-grouping only, didn't have DNA. I think on the list now, there'd be well over fifty that have been cleared by DNA.'

In other words, police have a DNA profile of the man who raped and murdered Suzanne Armstrong from the semen found under her body, but have been unable to find its 'match'. This has not been through lack of trying. In 2012, a second round of DNA tests were ordered for the eight men who had been the key suspects, in the hope that advances in forensic technology would lead to new information. All men had been cleared the first time this forensic methodology was used in this case, more than a decade earlier.

Suzanne's stepfather, Bruce Currie, said he and his wife, Eileen, had been told at the time that the original suspects were to be retested. 'He [Iddles] reckoned the DNA testing hadn't been done correctly in the first place. So they were redoing it . . . for about eight people, I think,' Mr Currie said. 'He said they had one more to do the last time I was talking to him.'

Police declined to confirm whether this testing was sparked by advances in DNA technology or because there were problems with the original samples.

Extensive testing was also conducted on voluntarily provided blood samples. Iddles, described as the 'lead investigator' at the time, said that a wide range of testing was done: thirty to thirty-five people were DNA-tested in total, including those key suspects. But even with the precise methodology and extraordinary scientific advances in forensics testing, none of the men involved in this second round was deemed a match to the DNA profile 'built' from the evidence retained from the murder scene.

Still, he and his team did not give up. 'While DNA testing has so far failed to uncover an offender, it has proven a useful tool in eliminating suspects,' he said.

A year on, in 2014, the veteran detective took a call from a woman who confessed the suspicions she had long held about a man now in his eighties. She had read about the latest technology and believed he should be DNA-tested. 'She said, "Listen, I don't know whether I'm right, but I've had this suspicion about a man who's now eighty-two," and she told me a long, long story,' Ron Iddles said at the time. 'And now what I need to do is to ultimately go and get his DNA.'

He did that, of course. But it was just another long, long story that came up short. The 82-year-old was cleared. No charges were laid, no arrest made. When Iddles finally retired in 2016, whoever killed the 'two Sues' was still at large. And the young women are never far from his mind.

CHAPTER 16

THE SCIENCE

RECENT ADVANCES IN forensic testing have been extraordinary. It's as if the unique combinations to unlock the world's most precious vaults are constantly being cracked.

But what is a DNA profile, exactly? And just how reliable is it? Considering how much a part of our legal and cultural landscape DNA testing has become, it is fascinating to trace its history.

DNA stands for deoxyribonucleic acid, the chemical that controls the structure of each cell, and carries the genetic information at the centre of our cells. Often tagged 'the blueprint of life', its existence has tantalised scientists for centuries.

In 1866, Augustinian monk Gregor Mendel was the first person to shed light on how genetic characteristics are passed down through generations. Although he is now widely acknowledged as 'the father of genetics', it took thirty years for his work on pea plants to be taken seriously. Essentially, he found that when a yellow pea plant was bred with a green, the offspring was always yellow – until the next generation. Way ahead of his time, the scientist coined the terms 'dominant' and 'recessive' in relation to genes.

Three years later, a Swiss chemist identified what he called 'nuclein' in the nuclei of human white blood cells, which we know now as DNA. Early the next century, Sir Archibald Edward Garrod linked Mendel's theories with a human disease, collecting family histories from patients. By the 1940s, scientists' understanding of the principles of inheritance had developed considerably: genes were known to be discrete units of heredity, as well as playing a role in metabolic functions. However, it wasn't until 1944 that deoxyribonucleic acid was identified as a 'transforming principle'.

Intriguingly, it was a woman, in this very male-dominated field, who conducted a significant portion of the research that eventually led to the understanding of the structure of DNA. Her name was Rosalind Franklin, and her role was to 'set up and improve the X-ray crystallography unit' at King's College in London. She worked with the scientist Maurice Wilkins and a postgraduate student, Raymond Gosling, and was able to produce two sets of high-resolution photographs of DNA fibres, described as 'the most beautiful X-ray photographs of any substance ever taken'.

From 1951, Franklin came close to discovering the structure of DNA. But fellow scientists Thomas Watson and Frances Crick gained some key information about her research from Maurice Wilkins, and used it to solve a puzzle that had baffled scientists for decades. In April 1953 they published a paper in *Nature* titled 'Molecular Structure of Nucleic Acids: A Structure for Deoxyribose Nucleic Acid', outlining their findings. In 1962, they were awarded a Nobel Prize, along with Maurice Wilkins. Although her photographs had been critical to their finding, Rosalind Franklin was not honoured, as the Nobel Prize committee claimed that only three scientists could share the prize.

In 1990, when the Human Genome Project – an international research effort to map the sequence of human DNA – got underway, DNA evidence was already being used in criminal investigations and trials around the world. By the time the Human Genome Project was completed in 2003, DNA profiling had become a staple of contemporary television drama, a little piece of science we all took for granted.

In a way, it's disconcerting to realise that only nine years after Suzanne Armstrong and Sue Bartlett were murdered, the first DNA evidence was presented in a criminal trial. It was a world-first that followed an accidental scientific discovery and would end up involving a whole town.

In 1984, geneticist Alec Jeffreys had made a remarkable finding during a failed experiment to study how inherited illnesses are passed down in families. Working at the University of Leicester, he had extracted DNA from cells and attached it to photographic film, which was then left in a developing tank. As *The Guardian* noted on the thirtieth anniversary of this milestone, 'once extracted, the film showed a sequence of bars: Jeffreys quickly realised that every individual whose cells had been used in the experiment could be identified with great precision. Furthermore, the technique could be used to determine kinship.'

After publishing his discovery, Jeffreys was asked to assist in cases where children were being denied British citizenship because immigration officials were disputing their genetic links to their parents. 'But DNA fingerprinting had yet to be used in a criminal investigation,' *Guardian* writer Ian Cobain noted. 'When Jeffreys gave his first talk about his discovery and suggested that it could be used to apprehend criminals, some in the audience had laughed out loud.'

Months later, his test helped free an innocent young man police had arrested for the murder of a teenager in Leicestershire. Initially taken aback by the results – 'one minute we got the guy, the next we've got jack shit', a senior investigator is reported to have muttered – police made an extraordinary leap of professional faith that led to an unprecedented step. Not content to officially embrace Jeffreys' DNA procedure, they used it to test all the men living in and around the neighbourhood. Letters were sent to every male born between 1953 and 1970 in the area, requesting a blood sample. Two testing centres were set up, and by the month's end, almost 1000 men had given samples. After eight months, 5511 men had given blood samples – only one had refused.

One man recorded as having provided a sample was 27-year-old Colin Pitchfork, a baker and a father of two. Three years earlier, he had been questioned about his movements on the evening of the murder. But a workmate confessed he had given a DNA sample for his colleague. 'Pitchfork had asked for this favour because he had already taken the test for a friend who had a conviction for indecent exposure when he was younger. Pitchfork had doctored his passport, inserting Kelly's photograph, and then driven him to the test centre at the school, waiting outside while the blood sample was taken,' the article noted. 'Six weeks later, one of the people in the pub relayed this conversation to a local policeman. Kelly was promptly arrested, and by the end of the day Pitchfork was also in custody ... he gave a detailed confession.' DNA evidence was used in the trial to secure his conviction.

That same year, 1986, the first DNA evidence was introduced in the United States court system, during the trial of a rape case in Florida. Here in Australia, it would take another three years for it to be employed: in 1989, Desmond Applebee was convicted of sexual assault after DNA found on the victim's clothes proved to be his. 'DNA profiling from blood and semen on the victim's clothes showed that there was one chance in 165 million that it was not his. After a period of attacking the police investigation, he changed his defence to one of consent. The jury ... had little difficulty ultimately in convicting him.'

Later that year, a Melbourne serial rapist, George Kaufman, pleaded guilty to several rapes after DNA evidence indicated that he was the perpetrator. His wife and daughter initially provided DNA samples, and he later provided a blood sample himself.

The fact that police had a DNA sample to match Kaufman against is actually a remarkable chapter in police history. As early as 1982, Tony Raymond, then the director of the forensic services centre with Victoria Police, had enough faith in the progress that forensic science would make in the next few years to order hundreds of samples from unsolved crime scenes to be stored in a special freezer at –70° Celcius. Everything – clothing, hair, semen and weapons – was stored in this freezer. When the technology to test the samples became available in Australia a few years later, Raymond's foresight was a boon to police.

In 1989, George Kaufman became the first person convicted due to those so-called 'freezer samples'. Found guilty of nineteen rapes, he also became the first person in Victoria to be jailed largely as a result of DNA evidence.

Given this successful adoption of DNA profiling, it is not surprising that Victoria was the first Australian jurisdiction to legislate for a DNA database in 1997. But however improbable it may seem, this database has not shed light on what happened inside 147 Easey Street. Nor has the National Criminal Investigation DNA Database (NCIDD), despite being available '24 hours, seven days a week to all Australian police agencies'. Under the jurisdiction of the Australian Criminal Intelligence Commission, this database now contains 'more than 1.2 million DNA profiles ... from samples collected by Australian police from crime scenes, convicted offenders, suspects, volunteers, items belonging to missing persons, and unknown deceased persons'.

When Chief Commissioner Graham Ashton became aware of the freezer store in late 2009, after he was appointed the lab's director, there were '1936 samples from the scenes of 582 unsolved crimes,' reporter Keith Moor wrote in 2017. Ashton said that DNA technology had advanced sufficiently to enable them to test the samples from the freezer. 'Since then, more than eighty rapists have been identified directly as a result ... None of them were suspects for the sex attacks prior to the samples being taken out of the freezer they had been stored in since the early 1980s,' Moor wrote. 'The results of the 1982 decision by Dr Raymond to store the samples ... have been spectacular. Comparing all 428 DNA samples obtained from the freezer with the just over one million DNA samples on the national DNA database resulted in 113 "cold hits" relating to 290 sex offences.'

A 'cold hit' occurs when samples in the national DNA database match DNA from the scene of an unsolved crime. A person who until then wasn't a suspect becomes one. DNA matches can also occur between crime scenes, revealing crimes committed by the same serial offender – even if previously no link had been identified between them.

Still, there is nothing to link the DNA from the Easey Street murderer to a suspect – yet.

The NCIDD was set up back in 2001, providing forensic experts and police with access to DNA profiles of convicted criminals, which they can match with samples taken from crime scenes and individuals. It allows all Australian state and territory catalogues to connect, so DNA profiles can be shared nationally.

According to Paul Gregoire and Ugur Nedim at Sydney Criminal Lawyers, the NCIDD held 830,000 DNA profiles in 2014, and its archive is constantly growing. 'Each year, the NCIDD conducts 68,000 attempts to match profiles on the database with crime scene DNA, and more than 72,000 comparisons from crime scene to crime scene.' This information can also be used internationally. 'In November 2014, Australian Justice Minister Michael Keenan announced the nation was entering into a pilot program with the UK, the US and Canada, enabling the international exchange of information.'

If this sounds Orwellian, it pales in comparison to what the New South Wales police minister proposed: that the national DNA bank store genetic samples from all newborns, which could then be accessed under a Supreme Court warrant and compared with crime scene DNA.

This illustrates how widely accepted the general concept of DNA profiling has become. There is a sense that it is infallible. It is certainly seen as the most accurate way of building a case around a suspect, even if other aspects of that case – motive and other crime-scene evidence – are less than convincing. Yet, as Gregoire and Nedim emphasise, 'while DNA matching is more reliable than many other forensic techniques, it is certainly not foolproof. DNA profiles have been incorrectly matched in several cases in the past. Samples have also been contaminated in the laboratory, and there have been cases where they've been wrongly labelled.'

They cite the example of Farah Jama, who was convicted in 2008 of sexually assaulting an unconscious 48-year-old woman in a nightclub. Even though there was no evidence placing Jama at the club on the night of the incident, samples taken from the woman's body were found to match his DNA. He was convicted on the strength of the DNA evidence and jailed for eighteen months before it was discovered that contamination occurred when forensic samples were taken from the victim. 'The Victorian Court of Appeal found that the officer who examined the woman had earlier taken samples from another woman in the same room, a person who had engaged in consensual sexual intercourse with Mr Jama.'

Could it be a possibility that the DNA profile from Easey Street that detectives have been working with for nearly two decades was contaminated in a lab, early on in the investigation?

A source close to the case is adamant that the exhibit box in which the DNA material collected at the Easey Street crime scene was stored, along with other items taken from the house, was 'lost' in police storage for at least a decade. If this allegation is true, was it due to sloppy management – a mislabelling of the box (or boxes), or a simple clerical filing error – or part of a plan to put the case on the backburner? If the evidence was hard to find, that theory seems to suggest, perhaps community interest in the murders would wane and criticism of detectives' lack of progress ease. If the box or boxes of exhibits *were* misplaced, is it far-fetched to ask if DNA samples stored within them could also have been mislabelled? Could this be why none of the eight original suspects for this double homicide has matched the police DNA?

It's not implausible. Even the most rigorous DNA enquiry can almost come undone. After four decades of tracking the man dubbed the 'Golden State Killer' – alleged to have murdered at least twelve people and raped forty-six women – early in 2017 detectives in the United States believed they had found him. Comparing DNA discovered at the crime scene against genealogy websites, they converged on a 73-year-old in an Oregon nursing home. He had no criminal record, had never been suspected of a crime, but he shared a rare genetic mutation found in only 2.3 per cent of Caucasians in the database. It was the 'closest match ever seen'. Not unreasonably, investigators suspected he could be the killer, or at least related to the killer.

A judge gave the necessary permission to obtain the nursing home resident's DNA, which he gave voluntarily. Further tests immediately ruled him out.

A year later, the DNA and genealogy websites dragnet led detectives to a second man, who fit the criminal profile of the killer they were hunting. He was also ruled out.

Months later, James Joseph DeAngelo was identified. 'In his case, authorities zeroed-in after locating a distant relative among GEDmatch.com's 850,000 genetic profiles. Investigators traced his family tree and surveilled [sic] him. They watched him discard his DNA in a public place, allowing them to obtain a sample,' the *Los Angeles Times* noted. 'DNA can be obtained from gum, a used cup, skin cells or fallen hair. Officials have not revealed what type of DNA sample they obtained from DeAngelo or how they got it – only that it matches the genetic evidence left behind after at least three rapes in Northern California and three killings in Orange County.'

Intriguingly, what's known as 'autosomal DNA testing' was first used to solve, at least in part, the Bear Brook murders in New Hampshire, in north-eastern America. They dated back to 1985. This means that, despite genuine civil liberty issues, police now have four precise DNA tests available to assist in cold cases: the main test, which looks for an identical DNA match; one that searches for maternal and paternal links, another that tracks immediate family members; and the astonishing 'auDNA' test that can 'see' 700,000 markers on a DNA sample and trace fifth and even fourth cousins.

This is what popular online sites such as Ancestry.com draw on for users determined to build detailed family trees or find long-lost relatives. It has also led to 'genetic genealogists' being able to help detectives try to solve some of the trickiest murder mysteries – like the four bodies found in two barrels in Bear Brook a couple of years ago.

Ancestry.com states that in 2017 it fielded thirty-four requests from police for DNA searches related to criminal cases, most from

Germany and the United States. Yet, as genetic analysis continues to revolutionise forensic detection, and police around the world are starting to employ these new tools to track down criminals via their family members, Australian authorities seem reluctant to step into this new frontier.

In July 2018, Victoria Police and the Australian Federal Police told *The Sydney Morning Herald* that they did not 'currently use online genealogy databases to help solve crimes'. Ancestry.com spokeswoman Alice Coulthard confirmed the service had yet to receive a DNA request from any law agency based in Australia.

If this much time and resourcing is to be spent on one cold case in Victoria, which one will it be? The oldest? The most violent? Who makes that decision?

And how reliable are the DNA samples from Easey Street, taken more than forty-two years ago? Experts seem to agree that, even if the exhibit boxes were misplaced, as long as the DNA material was stored properly – kept dry and out of direct sunlight and not housed in a plastic bag – it should be usable, and so legally 'safe'.

Can Sue's and Suzanne's families be confident that proper care has always been taken with this most crucial evidence? Several lawyers and at least one former investigator believe this is a significant question that must be addressed.

CHAPTER 17

THE REWARD

VICTORIA POLICE COMMANDER Doug Fryer turned to the cameras and microphones. 'Put yourself in the position of these families – imagine the grief you would feel never knowing. Do the right thing and help us bring the person to justice.'

Not long before Ron Iddles retired, Victoria Police took a major step. In a bid to generate new leads for their reinvigorated cold case team, eight rewards of $1 million each were announced.

They related to eight suspicious deaths and missing persons cases dating back to 1985. The cases included a woman killed while sunbathing at Rye, a woman strangled in her home at West Geelong, a woman found dead after taking a taxi home from a nightclub in Ballarat and a man shot with a high-powered hunting rifle in Bendigo.

All eight matters had 'been before the coroner, and our avenues of inquiry with the investigations have come to a stop', Victoria Police Commander Doug Fryer noted. Victoria Police were hopeful that the rewards would generate crucial information to help resolve the matters. 'There are people of interest in many of these investigations but we're asking the community and the public for assistance,' he told the media. 'We know there are people out there in each one of these eight cases who can come forward and provide that crucial piece of the puzzle to solve these crimes.'

Families of those murdered individuals spoke out publicly in support of the initiative. A woman named Donna, the daughter of Debbie Bunworth, who disappeared from Newport train station in September 1985 and was assumed to have met with foul play, said her family had lived for thirty-two years with the 'sadness of not knowing where she is or who is responsible for her disappearance'.

This $8 million reward bonanza made international headlines. It also refocused community attention on old murders not necessarily in the category of 'Victoria's most notorious', and so rarely in the news.

But offering rewards for the solving of serious crimes can be a slippery slope. Months earlier, police had made clear that the rewards system was being overhauled, after former police commissioner Ken Lay described the system as 'unnecessarily complicated'. Now, rewards were going to be based on the maximum penalty that could be handed down by the courts for the crime, with six levels within the new system. Level one included a maximum penalty of life imprisonment, and so came with a $1 million reward.

The approach, hailed by many families of victims in cold cases, led to national debate about the value of rewards generally. Do they elicit genuinely useful information? Or are they little more than an old-fashioned publicity stunt, a low-resource way for police to show they are doing their job, but offering little more besides?

A New South Wales law firm, Sydney Criminal Lawyers, argued that such rewards are 'ineffective' in solving crimes. Principal lawyer Ugur Nedim wrote that in England figures show that fewer than

2 per cent of people eligible for a reward claim it, and, locally, Crime Stoppers Australia estimates that only 6 per cent of its callers end up claiming a reward. Clearly it is not a key factor in people's decisions to come forward with information.

In fact, rewards are rarely paid out. None of the $14 million Victorian Police had earlier offered for information relating to forty-three different crimes has left police coffers. A 2009 investigation by ABC's *Lateline* found that over a ten-year period only two of seventy claims for rewards were ever paid. The first led to the arrest and conviction of notorious backpacker murderer Ivan Milat, and the second led to the arrest of Michael Gyder, who was convicted of killing nine-year-old Samantha Knight.

The main purpose of a reward, according to Nedim, is to offer 'comfort and hope to families of those who have been missing for years', showing that 'the community cares about their predicament'.

Ron Iddles would no doubt disagree with any suggestion that police lack integrity in terms of paying out rewards when solid information has led to arrests and convictions. But he is only too aware that this kind of incentive has not had the impact hoped for. 'In the past thirty or forty years, I think they've only paid out on two or three,' he muses.

It's not only Australian authorities wrestling with the legal and moral conundrum of whether to offer a public inducement to help solve crimes. In the United Kingdom, rewards are widely used, and linked to another contentious tactic authorities employ to stir compassion and engagement: police regularly use graphic images and interviews with desperate relatives to galvanise witnesses. 'The reason behind putting up the sum of money is straightforward – to create greater media opportunities to glean vital information and help solve crimes,' Nick Howe, former chief superintendent with Staffordshire Police and a criminologist at the University of Derby, told BBC News reporter Emma Hallett. 'In cases funded by the police – and therefore the taxpayer – cash rewards are more likely to be offered for "heinous types of crime" ... [cases] which cause moral outrage ... murder, elderly people that have been severely battered ... the ones that appeal to human sympathy and emotion.

'What the police don't want to do is contaminate evidence and the integrity of the investigation,' Howe said. 'If the person who is providing the information is actually a witness in the case, then the defence will, quite rightly, suggest ... the evidence has been tainted by the inducement of payment ... [Yet] if information can fast-track inquiries – bearing in mind most major inquiries/murder inquiries are very expensive ... I think you can argue it is good use of public money.'

Tim Passmore, police and crime commissioner in Suffolk, said there were 'few occasions' when offering a reward was the best way to solve a case. 'It would be very sad if a system were to evolve where people expected to be paid for providing evidence,' he told Hallett.

This debate brings up a vexed issue: what is the media's role and responsibilities in terms of cold-case inquiries? Obviously it's vital in getting the message out to the community when a reward is announced, and refreshing the public on details of a case. But how much follow-up should the media give these cases, as police sift through new information that comes in to them? How much can they give?

When it comes to cold cases, the relationship between police and the media seems to depend less on the detectives, who often want to engage with journalists, than on the attitudes of their superiors – a prevailing culture within police ranks about how 'useful' reporters can be to them as information gatherers. Victoria Police appear to take the stance that most reporters are of little use beyond the initial media call announcing a reward for the most recently 'exhumed' cold case. They hold their cards extremely close in terms of discussing active investigations with the media. Gone are the days a veteran reporter would be allowed to read through a police murder file, at police headquarters, as veteran crime writer Tom Prior and his colleague did more than two decades ago.

Unsurprisingly, Ron Iddles holds a different view. He sees strong working relationships with journalists as a vital tool in police work, and has praised the role of the media in publicising unsolved murders and other cold cases. 'The media has a big part to play in helping police get information to solve crimes,' he said before his retirement. 'Former Homicide Squad chief Paul Delianis said to me in 1980, "as a Homicide Squad investigator, Ron, you need the media and the media need you." That still holds true today.'

He cited one case as proof of this point. One of the early successes of Victoria's original cold case unit came from a tip following a story in the *Herald Sun* newspaper, which mentioned the unsolved rape and murder of six-year-old Bonny Clarke in 1982. A childhood friend of Clarke's read the article and revealed that she had always suspected a man who had been a boarder at the Clarke home, because he acted 'in a weird sexual way'. 'It turned out the lodger was the murderer and he was charged and convicted in 2004, after an elaborate undercover sting organised by Senior Sargeant Iddles and Homicide detective Tim Day. That sting led to a secretly taped confession … that he did it.' Iddles is convinced this would not have happened without that story being written.

In the public flurry that followed the eight cold cases suddenly given million-dollar 'bounties' – and two more that followed in 2016 – it was difficult to believe the horrific double homicide in Easey Street did not warrant this attention. Was it just too old to resolve? Or were authorities waiting for something?

With the forty-year anniversary of the murders looming, some veteran crime journalists – those who remembered the original reports of what had happened in the little house – wondered if it would be the next case to have a public reward posted.

They were right.

On 15 January 2017 – almost forty years to the day that Sue Bartlett's and Suzanne Armstrong's bodies were found in their Collingwood cottage – Homicide chief Mick Hughes, with Gayle Armstrong by his side, put the $1 million reward on the table.

The Easey Street case was hard to read about, even for journalists who had long been following it. So for a family member, attending the media conference to launch the reward must have been nigh on impossible to endure.

Nevertheless, Gayle Armstrong made the most of her time with the senior Homicide detective. Brave, heartbroken, determined, she called once more for the public's help in solving her sister's murder, so many years after that first appeal in 1977.

This time, she did not hold back. 'I hate to say it, but here's a million dollars,' she said, obviously well beyond frustrated. 'You can live the rest of your life in comfort – just say something!'

Journalists gathered for that press call at police headquarters were left with no illusions about how her family had been treated in January 1977. 'We weren't even interviewed,' she said in her usual clipped manner. 'We had to make an appointment to go down to the police station to speak to the police, which was really bad.'

This forced Homicide detective Mick Hughes to admit that the initial inquiry had been fraught, acknowledging it was now standard practice to interview the families of murder victims. But, despite 'the mistakes those guys may have made in the early days, I know all they want is this investigation to be solved, for the sake of both families'. He told reporters he did not believe that the perpetrator of so brutal a crime could go unnoticed. The killer, now believed to be in his sixties or seventies, was unlikely to have lived crime-free since 1977. 'Someone will know something about his behaviour or conduct that can point us to him.'

Police had a DNA profile of the murderer, and a list of 131 'persons of interest'. Forty-one of those had since died. 'We've made substantial inroads to the remainder of the people on those lists,' he noted.

But the original eight key suspects had been ruled out after DNA testing. Detectives currently working the case had no fresh leads. Perhaps because of this, Hughes called on anyone who had been questioned at the time of the first investigation to get in touch with them again now, via Crime Stoppers Victoria. 'If you're going to offer your DNA, we'll certainly do that. The only person who's got anything to hide here is the offender.'

The cost of retelling this story was evident when Gayle was asked by a reporter what it meant to her that police were still actively searching for her sister's killer. 'Everything, everything,' she said, trying not to break down. 'This reward should have been offered thirty-nine years ago and [the murders would] be solved and we wouldn't be doing all this now. With the DNA, even if this person is dead, you can now go to family members and find out that way if it was that person.' It was a plea from the heart.

News of the million-dollar reward had been broken by the *Herald Sun* newspaper hours before the media conference. According to its report, the existence of DNA left at the scene and advancements in forensic testing were critical factors in relaunching this probe. 'We have good DNA evidence and we obviously believe that's the key to the investigation,' Detective Inspector Hughes said. 'We haven't got a match. If we did, I'd be knocking on someone's door and making an arrest.'

He said the brutality of the murders had deeply affected the police investigating the case, not to mention the women's families. 'Every Homicide investigator who has worked on this case has been moved by the ferociousness of the attacks and wants it solved.' While the women's deaths had been linked to other murders over the years, no conclusive connection had ever been established. Depressingly, this echoed the fact that while there were several knives related to the case in police exhibit boxes, detectives were not convinced that any of them were the actual murder weapon.

Gayle's courage during this media launch did not waver. She told journalists that since her sister and her friend had died, she found watching the news too hard because it was 'all concerning people like me'. Yet, somehow, she still had faith in the police. 'I hear the miracles that they do and I think Suzanne will be next. They will do it, they will find this person.'

CHAPTER 18

THE THEORIES

FOR DECADES NOW, much has been made of one broad theory: that it would be impossible for a killer capable of two such vicious murders not to repeat the violence, and so come to police attention. The sexual element of the attacks, the debasement of Suzanne Armstrong's body, suggests to forensic psychologists an anger towards women that would be hard to control. Most detectives who have worked on this case have long believed the man or men responsible for murdering Suzanne and Sue must have killed again; they argue the perpetrators could not have controlled themselves.

For the past forty-two years, police have been on high alert for similar attacks. But as significant as the sexual violence towards Suzanne Armstrong, and the furious, frenzied nature of the stabbing of her friend was, perhaps the presence of sixteen-month-old Gregory Armstrong is equally important. Was the murderer's excitement heightened because the little boy was there too?

If a child being nearby *is* relevant to the psychological profile of this attacker, it certainly narrows down the number of attacks that can be compared to the double murder. In fact, there has really only been one other case that shares some of the same characteristics as

Easey Street, and that is the 1982 stabbing death of Jenny Rose Ng, a mother of four who lived in Richmond, a suburb next to Collingwood.

Some of the details of the 39-year-old's murder in her housing commission flat in Richmond are uncomfortably close to the double homicide in Collingwood, just a ten-minute walk away. Ng was murdered in a 'stabbing frenzy'. She was found by two of her young daughters, just seven and eleven years old, who had returned from school to have lunch with their mother and baby sister. Ng was lying face down in the living room after being stabbed thirty times. Her baby, unharmed, was sleeping in a cot in another room.

Police said the door to Ms Ng's apartment was unlocked, and she was found in her dressing gown, indicating that she either let him in, or perhaps knew the murderer and had given him a key. They also revealed that a neighbour had heard a man speaking in Cantonese that morning, as well as furniture being moved around the flat.

Born in China, Jenny Rose Ng had migrated to Australia as a girl. She had separated from her husband, the father of her four children: three daughters and a son. In 2012, on the thirtieth anniversary of her murder, her family and police tried to rally new interest in the case, with one of her now adult daughters saying she believed there were residents still living in the neighbourhood who could help catch her mother's killer. The daughter told reporters that she sensed there were people who knew something about her mother's death, or perhaps even saw something on that day. 'I just want them to recall the memory and come forward now. It's a long time later, but maybe they felt like they couldn't say anything before.'

Six years after this appeal and thirty-six years after Jenny Rose Ng died, no one has been charged with her murder. But in April 2018, a million-dollar reward was officially offered for information about this cold case, too.

Of course, there have been other stabbing murders in the forty-two years since Easey Street. None have compelled police to think there could be a link. But early on, they did eliminate one 'interesting' suspect who was certainly well known in the Collingwood vicinity: Neil Rowland Bugg.

Andrew Rule reported that a few years before Mark 'Chopper' Read died in 2013, he mentioned knowing Bugg in jail. 'Prisoners were wary of the volatile "Buggsy". They avoided waking him up because he would leap up and attack them. Most prisoners believed Bugg had done the Easey Street murders – and had been overlooked because of being arrested for another murder around the same time: supposedly a case of hiding in plain sight,' the report claimed.

Rule noted that Read's story fit with some intriguing facts. At 4.00 am on 1 January 1977, a constable called Ron Iddles was first on the scene at a car accident in Wellington Street, Collingwood. A vehicle driven by Peter Phillip Fergeus, a labourer from Epping, had run off the road: a back-seat passenger had cut his throat with a broken bottle while he was driving. 'The vigilant Iddles noticed blood on an onlooker's feet and told detectives,' Rule noted. 'It was Bugg, alias "Lester Hargreaves".'

Neil Bugg lived just a ten-minute walk away from where he killed Peter Fergeus 'in a senseless frenzy'. His home was, according to Rule, about 500 metres from 147 Easey Street.

Bugg was interviewed by police over the murder but released from custody before 10 January, the night of the Easey Street murders. He was arrested in Brisbane on 23 January, and extradited to face charges of murdering Fergeus. 'It's possible but unlikely he was asked to prove he wasn't in Melbourne on the night of the Easey Street murders.'

It was another red herring. Andrew Rule's story was passed on to detectives sometime around 2008. Investigators obtained Bugg's DNA, the crime reporter was told unofficially by police sources – and they presumably checked it against the Easey Street sample. There was no match.

Two days after the police press conference announcing the $1 million reward, there was a surreal twist in the story of the Easey Street murders.

Tess Lawrence, the journalist who had been at 147 Easey Street as the two families packed up Sue's and Suzanne's belongings, came forward with an astonishing revelation. She suggested that the Easey Street murderer might have called her after her article on the murders appeared in *The Herald*, back in 1977.

She detailed what happened on the website *Independent Australia*, where she is a contributing editor-at-large. The piece began with a dramatic set-up:

> I could smell their blood in the hallway. I remember I could smell the fear. I could almost taste it. I could hear my own inner screams and sensed theirs echoing in that desolate

> silence where lurk the ghosts of bleak tragedy and unnatural death at the hands of our own species ... Both sides of the narrow hallway walls were splattered with what seemed litres of blood. And what looked like macabre wallpaper stencilled in blood by the palms, hands and fingers of someone desperately trying to defend themselves from the maniacal and frenzied repeated stabbings of a cold-blooded and ruthless killer ...

She was at the house at the request of police, she noted. It was hoped that an article might encourage someone to come forward with information.

After recapping the current state of the investigation and the announcement of the reward, she revealed the chilling aftermath of her 1977 article. 'My ... article, if I remember rightly, detailed much of the murder crime scene, including descriptions of the sitting room, surrounds and objects in the room,' she wrote.

> I hoped for a response ... someone always knows; someone always suspects.
>
> But then I got a spooky phone call. It scared me. There was a male voice on the other end. Somehow, it was different to the other calls. He started to go through my article and dissect it.
>
> Then he started criticising the fact that I hadn't been so observant after all – that I had left things out about a record player I'd mentioned – specifically the name of a record.
>
> He was right. A chill went up my spine. I had indeed left out details about some of the records. Deliberately.

> He then mentioned objects in the house that I hadn't mentioned at all. But I didn't let on. While I tried to keep him talking, I wrote a note and passed it to a colleague asking him to contact the switchboard and see if they could trace the call.

Tess Lawrence reported the caller was derisory of her lack of observation and 'strangely annoyed – the unidentified record (an LP) seemed to mean something to him'.

While he would not give Lawrence his name, he implied that he worked in signals at Victoria Barracks. When Lawrence asked if they could meet, 'his attitude changed a bit': 'He said he would call me back. My recall is that he ended the conversation abruptly.'

The high-profile journalist swiftly let detectives know of her call, but is not sure if they followed up on it. Four decades later, she still hasn't been told. Her final questions in the article are almost plaintive. 'Was the caller the murderer? Did he *know* the murderer? Was he calling on behalf of the murderer?'

Three good questions, all unanswered.

And it is still not clear what police made of the call. Did they try to track it, or just write it off as a 'nutter' trying to impress a well-known reporter?

The exchange still unnerves her. 'I made a list of what was on the record player and the other records that were near it, without their sleeves. But I deliberately kept that out of the story,' she recounts. Whoever was on the line definitely 'cited the record that was on the record player at the time'.

Does she really think the murderer had listened to music while he was in the house? 'I felt that the person looked at the records …

and picked up one of them,' Lawrence says. She reveals that her old notes are in safe-keeping in a bank, and while she still won't name the record that was on the turntable at Easey Street, 'It wasn't "Helter Skelter", I can tell you that' – grim reference to the Beatles' song that American cult leader and murderer Charles Manson claimed as inspiration.

Tess Lawrence asked police if they fingerprinted the records that were out of their covers. It's another unanswered query, and one too many for the venerable journalist. She is calling for an inquiry into the police handling of the Easey Street investigation over the past four decades.

CHAPTER 19

THE REASSESSMENTS

ONCE THE MILLION-DOLLAR reward was posted, police ranks closed around the newly reactivated cold case. Beyond the media event, detectives were reticent to engage with reporters about this high-profile double homicide.

Most covering the announcement of the reward were too young to have witnessed the original media coverage of Sue and Suzanne's murders. If they were interested enough to look beyond the summary of the case the police gave, they would have had to search through the scattered newsprint reports still available online or skimmed microfiche in the state library for a more complete picture – reading stories of two young women killed in a city they didn't quite recognise, given the physical and cultural changes that have occurred over time.

And even if they had done this, so little was known. There was no public profile of the man who stabbed the women to death, no recent attempts to publicly re-examine the scene of the crime to jog the city's collective memory. So Sue and Suzanne's deaths seemed trapped in an era long gone: if detectives had any fresh information that could help reignite the community's involvement in helping to find the killer, they were unwilling to reveal it. For a generation brought up on television procedural dramas such as *Cold Case*, *CSI* and *Without a Trace*, this seemed an odd tactic, a missed opportunity.

Professor Debbie Kirkwood, Australia's most prominent academic expert in domestic violence and homicide, has studied the Easey Street case in some detail. She believes she can identify some of the personality traits of the assailant. Like every expert observer who has examined the murders through the years, she believes that Suzanne Armstrong was the attacker's target. 'It's very different to homicide involving intimate partners. The extreme viciousness, the sexualised and repeated, frenzied nature of the assaults make it seem that the sole motive was rape and murder by a man with extreme hatred of women, rather than a personalised desire to punish her because of jealousy or relationship problems.'

She initially felt that the murderer must have been one of Suzanne's partners, but the more she examined the case, the more that seemed unlikely. 'At first, I thought maybe he could have been a boyfriend or ex-boyfriend, because it so often is – or even a guy that she rejected, which might account for the anger and sexualised nature of the attack. But it is so extreme and so full of hate and sickness that surely that would have to be a big coincidence that she just happened to piss off a complete psychopath. This is such an unusual crime in its extremity and hatred that I think it is more likely a Peter Dupas kind of person, who somehow knew of Suzanne and where she lived.

'Maybe he lived in the neighbourhood or was somehow connected to someone who knew them. So the motive seems to be extreme sexual violence and less a kind of jealous boyfriend. A jealous boyfriend probably wouldn't have shown such a degree of hate for the other woman, who also appears to have been brutally stabbed – repeatedly, even though she wasn't sexually assaulted.'

Professor Kirkwood also has some sympathy for the police working on the double murder case back in 1977. 'I do wonder if the fact that two women having the same name may have added a challenge to the investigation and all subsequent thinking about the case, because it is so easy to get confused and miss things because of it.

'When you're looking at evidence, it's often quite difficult, because it's very abstract: you've got the different rooms, you've got the different women, you've got different evidence relating to the women. Even just for them thinking it through, it might have been a bit harder given they both had the same name, and I guess some mistakes could have been made as a result of that.

'It's those first few days, isn't it, that are really critical for trying to solve these sorts of cases ... maybe something was confusing or overlooked.'

Kirkwood is also unconvinced that necrophilia was a significant factor in this attack. 'If it's not someone close to her or known to her, then it moves into an area that I am not an expert in. But, you know, I personally think the fact of the way her body was left doesn't necessarily mean that the motive was to rape a dead person. I think that it's quite possible that she did die as a result of the assault fairly quickly and then he wanted to continue with his intention to sexually violate her. So he moved her legs apart, and because she was dead, she stayed that way.'

In other words, Debbie Kirkwood suggests, it didn't matter to Suzanne's killer whether or not she was alive when he had 'intercourse' with her.

On this point, another expert from a different field disagrees.

An internationally respected criminologist who looked into the case specifically for this book argues that, while the attacker's original intent might have been to engage Suzanne Armstrong in consensual sex, he came to the house armed with a knife. Once she refused his advances and started to fight him, he killed her quickly.

But the way he did so, stabbing her three times in the chest, suggests that he was sexually aroused by the violent act. The criminal profiler, who is unwilling to be identified here for fear of alienating Homicide police, says the murderer could have had a condition called paraphilia, which is characterised by abnormal sexual desires and typically involves extreme or dangerous activities.

This could explain his actions if he entered the house knowing Suzanne wasn't alone, that both her son and Sue Bartlett were there that night too. If this was the case, he probably knew that Sue was either in her room or at the other end of the house – in the kitchen or backyard of the property – when he entered. This made the whole scene potentially dangerous for him.

The profiler makes an even more startling claim. He believes that Suzanne's body was moved and posed after she died, and that her killer cleaned the blood from her wounds before having sex with her corpse. He suggests that she was lying on her stomach for some time before being turned over on her back. 'Surely that would leave smear marks of blood on her body, as she's then moved towards the door? So it seems likely that she was cleaned up at some point.'

His theory could explain the small pool of blood that was found near Suzanne's head and shoulder, as noted in the crime scene report, as well as her relatively unbloodied body, captured by the crime scene photographer.

For this expert, who has worked with police in investigating homicides nationally and internationally, it's almost impossible to 'profile' the Easey Street murderer because so little was gleaned about him from the crime scene during the original investigation. Did he take anything that belonged to either woman away from the house? Did he leave anything behind, something no one noticed at the time? It's never been determined – or if it has, this information has not been revealed publicly.

But the profiler is certain this was a double homicide, not a serial killing. 'There's two ways to look at it,' he explains. 'If we take the perspective that he's attacking Suzanne, but Susan interrupts him, then yeah – he certainly wouldn't have known she was there and the frenzied attack on her becomes more about his anger, and retaliation that she's interrupted him.

'But the alternative is that actually we're reading the situation wrong and he knew both victims *were* there and may not have expected Sue to approach as quickly – or he may have figured he could have overwhelmed Suzanne without her friend interfering.

'But I don't think that's the case. I think it's much more likely he either didn't realise she was there, or when the attack started to take place he didn't realise the implications of her being there.'

These are subtle, significant nuances in a terrible crime. But the way in which Sue Bartlett was attacked also confuses any 'perfect picture' of the killer. Her body was not cleaned, nor was she sexually violated after she was driven to the floor in the hallway.

This makes it hard to apply even the American Federal Bureau of Investigation's long-debated classification system of 'organised/disorganised' serial killers to this assailant. First introduced by special agents working at the FBI's training academy at Quantico to investigate sexually sadistic murders, the distinction was relied on for years to differentiate sexual homicides and also types of arson. But over the past decade in particular, it has been deemed too broad to be effective.

According to an article written by a UK team and published in the journal *Psychology, Public Policy and Law*, special agent Robert Ressler and his colleagues distinguished between organised and disorganised offenders 'on criteria that they claim can be drawn from an examination of the crime scene, the victim, and forensic reports':

> Ressler et al claimed that '... facets of the criminal's personality are evident in his offense. Like a fingerprint, the crime scene can be used to aid in identifying the murderer'. They proposed that offenders' behavioural and personality characteristics can be determined from evidence at a crime scene. This 'fingerprint' is proposed to take one of two distinct forms, either organised or disorganised.
>
> The organised offender is described as leading an orderly life that is also reflected in the way he commits his crimes. Highlighting some proposed characteristics, he is claimed to be of average to high intelligence, socially competent and more likely than the disorganised offender to have skilled employment.

> It is also claimed that he is apt to plan his offenses, use restraints on his victim and to bring a weapon with him to commit the murder and to take the weapon away with him from the crime scene.

In contrast, the disorganised killer left behind 'an overall sense of disorder and suggests little, if any, pre-planning of the murder. The disarray ... may include evidence such as blood, semen, fingerprints and the murder weapon.'

Even a cursory glance at the Easey Street crime scene indicates the murderer displayed a 'mixed' set of traits, both organised and disorganised. More helpful, perhaps, is Robert Keppel and Richard Walter's 'revised classification model for understanding sexual murder'.

This team came up with four new classifications to help homicide detectives better 'see' evidence at crime scenes: power assertion, power reassurance, anger retaliation and anger excitation. According to the international criminologist who has now studied the case, the Easey Street perpetrator displayed characteristics of the anger retaliatory rapist and murderer.

In such scenarios, the rape is planned 'and the initial murder involves overkill. It is an anger-venting act that expresses symbolic revenge on a female victim ... dynamically, the rape-homicide is committed in a stylised violent burst of attack for the purposes of retaliation, getting even and revenge on women'.

This kind of killer 'may have some kind of ruse to get inside the victim's house, but once the victim is isolated, he confronts her. Armed with a barrage of accusations, he responds to the victim's denial of him by hitting her in the mouth and about the face. As the assault becomes more combative, the aggressor may use weapons of opportunity (knives etc) to brutalise the victim ... Regardless of whether (she) is alive or dead, the assault continues until the subject is emotionally satisfied.'

Chillingly, this offender transfers the blame of the murder onto the victim and so 'does not experience any sense of guilt; accordingly, he does not own any feelings of wrongdoing. In fact, quite the contrary is true. That is, he can develop a sense of sentimentality over the victim and help search for the victim with tears in his eyes.'

As part of this particular suspect profile, the paper touched on another telling point about the offender's behaviour, indicating that 'his free-floating anger is the cause of many difficulties with authority. Mentally, his unpredictable behaviour may have resulted in his being referred to a mental health worker.'

All of this makes sense to the visiting criminologist, who believes it helps to at least start to build a general perspective on the man who became the 'Easey Street murderer' – perhaps unwittingly. 'I don't have the view that this is some homicidal maniac psychopath that the movies like to depict, who breaks in and absolutely "overkills" these women,' he says. 'I think it's much more the case that Suzanne Armstrong was the target for whatever reason and, given the crime scene, I think there's probably a past there. There's a background there, there's already a resentment that's built up, especially if he's carrying a knife with him, which seems likely.

'I think there's a certain intent – that perhaps he was just going to rape her or try to force her to have sex. At that point, she starts to react aggressively in a way he wouldn't have expected.' At this point, the profiler says things start to get out of his control, as well as Suzanne's. 'Not that he didn't mean to stab her, but I think there could have been an argument [and] that he didn't mean to kill that night, so much as threaten her and rape her.

'Then Susan Bartlett becomes aware of what's going on, tries to come to the rescue – at which point everything's starting to fall apart and the frenzy takes over. The anger, the rage he's probably feeling from being rejected . . . by Suzanne, the feeling he's about to be found out and caught by the housemate who he may or may not have thought was in that night becomes overwhelming.'

The murders only make sense if they were unplanned, he argues. 'What we see sometimes with disorganised killers is they don't have much of a plan so when things start to fall apart, we get "overkill" – and "overkill" is usually thought of as an emotional reaction. It can sometimes be a kind of self-preservation fear. You can imagine the archetypal hitman who makes "one shot to the head, one shot to the heart" and leaves the scene of the crime, because they know anatomy and that's all you need. But what we sometimes see with people who are new to killing is this obliteration, because they want to take no risk of someone surviving.

'In this case, I think it's more about rage: perhaps he was known to the victims. I certainly think that's the case for Armstrong, which makes it likely that Bartlett knew him too. At this point, the killing becomes a factor of self-preservation, right? There's no risk of either of these women surviving and identifying him.'

Sadly, that part of this theory is indisputable.

CHAPTER 20

THE HOUSE

TODAY, EASEY STREET is part of Melbourne's hip, inner-city scene, its Smith Street end home to radio station PBS FM and three decommissioned trams that sit atop the roof of End to End's three-storey building. Opposite, the Token Artists team, professional agents for a stable of performers that includes Wil Anderson, Judith Lucy, Charlie Pickering and Dave Hughes, is located in an old factory that's been repainted many times over and now boasts their motto 'Excellence through guesswork'. A 'coffee alley' services the vibrant hub of local businesses that still includes A1 Drive Shafts and Timber and Veneer Boards just around the corner.

Closer still to number 147, there's a small children's park, not far from the Gold Street Children's Centre. But the house now sits on its own, its 'twin' at number 149 demolished long ago to make way for a car park for workers at the health clinic.

When Sue and Suzanne moved in, of course, it was a more rugged patch of town, a 'suburb with a history', where houses still nestled alongside low-rise factories, and the shadows cast by characters from Frank Hardy's *Power Without Glory* were still visible to many who had grown up or worked alongside them. Even students and young couples looking for cheap housing had yet to properly embrace Collingwood's workers' cottages and its rather scruffy outlook. Its small 'shotgun shacks', with slab-concrete backyards, were not as appealing as the wider streets and 'happy hippy culture' of Carlton and Fitzroy, which were also much closer for those studying or working at the University of Melbourne or RMIT.

For six years after the murders, 147 Easey Street stood empty, a lonely, silent contrast to the busy neighbourhood that started to blossom around it.

Unsurprisingly, given the enormous media coverage the double homicide had received and frequent references to the ongoing police inquiry within the local neighbourhood, the owner who had rented the property to the 'two Sues' found it impossible to find new tenants. Peter Demeris had bought the house as an investment property in 1976 for $19,500, and eventually sold it privately in 1983.

'It was difficult to sell because of what had transpired. It was fresh in people's minds,' Demeris would say decades later, when the house was sold again. 'It had that stigma to it, and obviously we sold it at a discounted figure.'

The new owner retained the house for nearly three decades. But they renovated it extensively, according to historian and neighbour Hugh Parry-Jones. 'In 1988, '89, the owner's got tradies in and they ripped up every bit of timber in the place,' he says, shaking his head. 'The house now sits on concrete slabs in every room.'

Seeing that the old wood was going to be laid to waste, the resourceful local decided to stockpile it for future use. 'So I piled all the skirting boards and the floor timber in the back alley that runs up to our house.'

Eventually, it was transformed into furniture and sold at the Fitzroy Craft Market. 'A guy came and got it and that's what he did with it, made furniture out of it. I told him its "history", about what had happened in the house it had been in. But he was really just interested in the old wood.

'I have a letter rack on my kitchen bench that he made. A bit strange, I guess. But there it is.'

It's not the only unusual thing to have happened in and around the house. After the renovation, the workers' cottage was rented by Dennis Gentry, who allowed a young documentary team to film inside the house as they interviewed him for an online documentary they posted in June 2011.

Part of the series *Vice Cool City*, the short, two-part video described the property as 'home to one of the most infamous crimes in Australia'. In it, Gentry maintains he didn't know about the murders when he moved in, eleven years earlier. 'I suppose it would have helped to actually know upfront that it was the house, because it would have explained a lot of the strange looks and notes that we used to get in the letterbox – and people driving past and slowing down and taking photos,' he told interviewer Natalie Harris. 'I mean, things used to go bump in the night and scare the living shit out of me ... [but] I think over time, I started relaxing into it and enjoying the house.'

He probably should have realised there was a reason 'the rent was really good' and 'the owners were having problems getting tenants'. But he, his three dogs, his cat and his flightless cockatoo weathered the obsessive, sometimes creepy interest their home continued to generate.

One early-morning visitor was particularly vexing. 'We were in bed and it's about three o'clock in the morning and someone's knocking on the front door,' he said. 'And there's this guy and he's pissed as a newt. I just told him to go away. 'But he says, "No, no, no, I know who they are." 'And I say, "Go away or I'll phone the police." And he says, "I want you to ring the police." I asked, "Why?" He responded, "Because I know who the murderer was."'

Dennis Gentry called police, who came to the house and told the man to leave. He did, only to return half an hour later. This went on three or four times before he eventually went away for good.

More intriguing is a note written in black texta that was left in letterboxes in Easey Street by an anonymous source. Senior criminologist Dean Wilson was a resident in the street at the time, lecturing at Monash University. Now a professor of criminology at the University of Sussex, he was interviewed by the team of young documentary-makers nearly a decade ago. 'This strange note that was written in black texta pen claimed that the actual perpetrator of the crime had died in Larundel Psychiatric Hospital sometime in the early 1990s, before the hospital was closed down,' he said on camera. 'No way to really test the veracity of that claim, though I must say it was a rather uncomfortable feeling to get that note and to be sort of drawn into the drama.'

New Zealander Wilson came to know Collingwood well, especially Easey Street. 'I lived in Easey Street twice during my years in Melbourne,' he says. 'Once in 1998–99 and then again from 2004 to 2010, when I owned a place. The note was dropped into the letterboxes when I was living at 100 Easey Street, so [that was] 2004–2005.'

Looking back on the letterdrop more than ten years later, he is now convinced there was credibility in what was being alleged. 'At the time, [the author] just seemed like a nut job,' he recalls. 'But now I think about it, there was a plausibility to what was being said in the note ... It's someone who's very passionate about the murders; it's someone who feels a connection to the murderer. The thing that was pretty creepy at the time was that it felt it had been sent to me. But now, on reflection, I think it was a letter drop and I suspect someone in the street still has a copy.'

As it turns out, he is correct. One copy does still exist, saved by long-term Easey Street resident Andrew Muir. In rather shaky capitals, it reads: 'Larundel Hospital protected Anthony Thomas Christie the Easey Street murderer for years. Sgnd, Peter Thomas Collier.' In the top right-hand corner, Muir has written the date: '25-11-05'.

Close neighbour Susy Potter is another who recalls the note – vividly. She moved into Easey Street five years after the murders, yet 'the street was still abuzz'. She pinned her copy to her message board and 'it was there for years ... The implication was, "I'm sitting on all this information and I'm going to blow it up – and if you want to help, contact me."'

That's certainly what Peter Collier seems to have been trying to do, reaching out to Easey Street locals, as well as to the Armstrong family the year before. At the very least, he was dogged in promoting his theory about the case. If Collier was right and the killer was a patient at Larundel 'for years', it could help to explain why police failed to get a match with their DNA sample – and why no other murders in Australia seems to have mirrored what occurred that night in Easey Street on 10 January 1977.

Forty-two years after Sue and Suzanne's deaths, their little house looks different. Like most in the street, it's been extensively renovated, the third bedroom knocked out to enlarge the living room, and repainted inside and out so that it blends in with the rest of contemporary Collingwood, no longer the poor part of Melbourne's inner-city suburbs. Real-estate prices have boomed in and around Easey Street over the last decade, and number 147 has changed hands twice since Peter Demeris sold it back in 1983.

Still, there's an ominous sense about the property, especially for long-term neighbours – and there probably always will be. The murders might have taken place more than a generation ago, but criminologist Dean Wilson finds it hard to believe that anyone wants to live in the house, even today. 'It's an iconic property in Melbourne, that's for sure. It definitely is ... [but] I don't know who would want to live in the house, I really don't,' he says, from halfway around the world. 'Even when I lived in the street, I used to walk past it and be surprised there was anyone willing to be in it.'

Some of Melbourne's real-estate agents have learnt the hard way the challenges of marketing the property. *The Age* reported in August 2011, 'More than 100 people turned up for the sale [of the property] ... many of whom proved more interested in visiting than buying the site of what is still regarded as one of the city's most shocking crimes.'

Weeks before the auction, the real-estate agent's marketing campaign had drawn fire from a victims' support group, which claimed the sales pitch was disrespectful, taking particular issue with the wording of advertisements that referred to its place in Melbourne's 'folklore'. 'Two girls were murdered there, a young boy lost his mother. [The families] still haven't had any closure because no one has ever been found,' said Bruce Kimball, from Support After Murder, who described the property's marketing as 'absolutely disgusting'.

Agents Nelson Alexander denied trying to capitalise on the property's notoriety, but did change 'folklore' to 'history' after media coverage about it. 'We were trying to fulfil disclosure obligations. We were trying to do it as discreetly as we could and be very, very sensitive to the history of the house,' agent Bill Batchelor said. 'Under consumer laws, agents must disclose that a murder or violent crime has occurred in a property when asked a direct question, but do not have to volunteer the information. But even with the crime more than three decades in the past, the property still had to be put on the market at a reduced price.'

Even so, the agents were happy with the result. The small Victorian terrace sold under the hammer for $571,000. '[The history] didn't seem to make much of an impact at all today,' said auctioneer Arch Staver. The new owner, a young woman, declined to be interviewed.

Four years later, the house came under the auctioneer's hammer again, selling for $1.095 million. This time, the agents copped criticism from locals for not mentioning the property's past. Certainly, the online copy steered clear from provocation:

> Enjoying a revitalised identity with a contemporary makeover while retaining its period lustre, this classic brick Victorian boasting a fresh neutral colour palette presents an excellent opportunity to secure a slice of the increasingly

> popular and tightly held inner city. With high ceilings and gleaming polished concrete floors, this refurbished home comprises 2 generously proportioned bedrooms with pure wool carpets and BIRs, living room with adjacent dining serviced by a well-appointed kitchen, refreshed bathroom and large courtyard/garden with excellent scope to extend. Exceptionally positioned in Collingwood's eclectic lifestyle precinct, the home is conveniently located to Victoria Park train station, buses, trams and the delights of Smith St.

Four decades later, it was a sensible approach. But long-time Easey Street residents still had qualms. 'I don't know what the right thing to do is here,' one reflected, months after the house was sold. 'But it just doesn't seem right to ignore what happened to those two girls.'

Despite the changing Collingwood streetscape, for many older residents still living in Easey Street, the morning the bodies of Suzanne Armstrong and Susan Bartlett were taken away from their rented property never seems that far away. Some memories can never be lost, even after four decades.

Andrew Muir has lived in the same house for forty-four years, and he remembers 13 January 1977 as the 'very hot day' that police descended on his street. 'They were always up there, on the roof. They were always coming in and out. Every time I'd go out [on the street], they seemed to be coming and going – and for quite a while after.'

Like many of his neighbours, he was comfortable in the street before the murders: he felt at home in Collingwood, and saw its potential long before the first hint of a real-estate boom. He bought the property in Sackville Street that abutted his house, to create a unique property of considerable value, with two matching 'Singapore cottages', originally imported in the 1850s, bookending his original home, which sits in the middle of the two blocks.

'I salvage them,' he says. 'I'm an amateur builder. I used to recycle furniture and building materials – it was just an extension of that, really.'

Andrew, who looks like a wiry Leo Sayer, has a unique perception of his precinct, considered 'undesirable' when he first moved in, though it did boast 'reasonable blocks'. 'It *wasn't* desirable. I mean, I bought for the house and garden really.' Like Hugh Parry-Jones, he has a sense of curiosity about the history and the planning of the suburb around him, especially the alleyways that twist through the streets. 'I'm interested in the lane layouts, and I hate it when they get blocked off. Very annoying.'

He doesn't think the street changed all that much in the aftermath of the murders. 'It wasn't all that friendly [before]. But then, I'm insulated here. I was never much a part of it, although if there was someone that I got on with, there would be a friendship while they were there. There've been a few over the years.'

There were also neighbours he did not get on with, and it's fair to say that one or two regard him, not unkindly, as eccentric. Yet while those in the street did not have a collective theory about who the murderer was, Andrew Muir always had two suspects in mind. He believed he knew two men police should have spoken to at the time, one who lived quite close by. 'Everyone has their theories. Mine was just, "How would it be if it was a guy who lived close to me at the time?" He was a very awkward piece of work,' he says. 'He'd scrounge some things from the empty old boot centre [at the end of the street], next to the health centre that was being developed at the time. Once, I was in his house – we must've been getting on at the time – and he showed me this set of Bentwood chairs that were all connected. I said, "Oh, you got them up there!" He said, "No, no, no!" He just lied. He always lied. Unusual. He used to put it on some of his tenants, he'd put the hard word on them.'

He knows this is drawing a long bow. Nevertheless, he mentioned it to the two female police officers who came to his house in January 2018 to conduct a DNA test. Forty-two years later, it seemed they were widening the scope of their inquiries – ten doors up the street.

'A couple of "lady cops!"' Andrew says with a laugh. 'Yes, I gave them DNA and spoke with them. I got the disc back. You may want to borrow it.'

The police made a copy of the recording of the DNA test being done and the conversation that took place in his kitchen, with his wife present, while it was happening. They mailed it to him about a week after their visit. Or so they thought. In fact, they mailed *a* disc to him – just not the right one. He claims they sent him a copy of another DNA test being done with a man who suggested they investigate Andrew as a possible 'person of interest'. It made disconcerting, if compelling, listening.

'I played it,' he recalls. 'They'd given me one of some other guy, who I'd actually done work for in my days of restoration. He was telling them about a guy who lived here and his house went from one street to the back and the next. That's me! It's just a hell of a coincidence.

'Then I figured it out. They'd been to see him before me. Does that make sense? But it wasn't that they came here because of what he said, and I don't know if they even would've absorbed the fact that it was me.'

Andrew knows the name of the man on the recording and believes he knows where he lives in Melbourne. But he decided against tracking him down to discuss the matter. 'I thought of ringing him, I would've tried to ring him, but he's not in the phone book. So how's that, eh?'

The police eventually realised they had mixed up the discs, and a detective dropped by to give him the correct recording and retrieve the one that had been mistakenly sent. 'He came in, in a bit of a rush. I try to gabble on with my theory – you know, the guy next door – [but] he just swapped the discs over. He was in a big hurry, he didn't want to stick around.'

Before the detective left, Andrew managed to regale him with his second theory. 'At the time I thought, *how would it be if it was this person?* There was a guy living down in Hoddle Street in a nice old house. I had a friend who'd tried to buy the contents of his truck, it was like a caravan truck. Anyway, this guy apparently got into some awful trouble and ended up in Queensland in some sort of lunatic asylum. I used to think, *well, he just lives down the road, he's a bit funny* ... so I mentioned that. He was my number-one choice!'

Yet as the detective was heading out, he told the Muirs that the man they were still hunting for the Easey Street murders could well have died in the preceding forty years. 'That's what [he] said. Yes, he just said, "We think he might be."' Dead.

Artist Steve Cox has an entirely different perspective of Easey Street. Born in London, he spent most of his childhood in Sussex before his family made the 'fairly traumatic' move to Tasmania in 1968. 'For the first six months, I couldn't understand what people were saying,' Steve says with a laugh, in a café not far from bustling Richmond train station. But after a couple of years, the family moved to the mainland, and the Australian dialect began to make more sense.

The budding painter enrolled at the Victorian College of the Arts in 1978. 'Which was the year I moved into Easey Street,' he recalls. 'I moved into this student house which was diagonally across the road from the "murder house". I didn't realise that was the street I was moving into, and then suddenly people were talking about it in the street – and kids would sort of run past [the] spooky house!'

Unlike several long-term residents, who maintain that the street didn't change much after the women were killed, Steve remembers a lingering apprehension even twelve months later. 'At the time, there was a milk bar on the corner of Hoddle and Easey Street. I think they were a European couple who ran it. I think they might have been Greek? They would talk about the murders a lot . . . They remembered it very, very dramatically and they would say how horrible it was.

'People in the street were still shocked by it at the time. I think there was a sense of, it could happen to anyone, in anyone's house. I think they were shocked by the seeming randomness of it and the fear that it could occur again in the street – which was unlikely. I would tell people, "That's not going to happen again." But there was a sense that they felt personally threatened and frightened still.'

The milk bar is not there anymore, nor the service station across Hoddle Street that the artist suggests provided another layer of intrigue. 'It was a big all-night service station. Speed was sold there. Not to us – I wasn't really aware of it, I was a bit naive as a twenty-year-old. We used to go across and play pool. We had no money, so I'd often go over with a bowl of cereal and eat my cereal in there at night. And people would come in all the time and do these little sorts of deals, and later on it dawned on me, they were selling speed or whatever! I think it was speed.'

Some of the locals he got to know talked about the 'two Sues' and knew them well enough to still openly grieve about what had happened to them, twelve months on. 'The milk bar people certainly knew them, they'd come in all the time. I think we got the sense that they were quiet, friendly, happy-go-lucky girls. That was always my understanding, which made the crime so shocking to the people in the street. The sense was that they didn't have any enemies and they were just going about their business. They were just ordinary girls – with a son, yeah.'

Living in his ramshackle student house for eighteen months, Steve Cox realised the murders of Suzanne Armstrong and Susan Bartlett had a major impact on his art. It wasn't the first time so dark a subject had compelled him; he had previously focused on the Moors murders in England. 'I was interested in the abhorrent psychology; what makes somebody decide to become a murderer? Having done that, they can never again re-join society, having made that step. They are always outside of society, and humanity, really. And what does somebody do once they've taken that step?'

He has no special knowledge of the double homicide at 147 Easey Street. But he wonders if the murders were truly random or 'part of a series of murders that someone was embarking on'. If so, he's fascinated by the 'for want of a better word, artistic' nature of the crime scene. 'In serial killings, there are always things that they do which are just pertinent to them, the arrangement of things or things they leave or things they take. And that was interesting to me. I didn't even have any images of the actual house, but I had images of this series [of paintings] I was thinking about: rooms, spaces where something awful had happened. I was very interested in the idea of this badness that comes in and affects something drastically, totally, and then moves out and nobody knows what it is. Does that make sense?'

The paintings and pictures that Easey Street inspired became part of Steve's student portfolio at VCA. But not much of it has survived the past four decades. 'People say to me, "How can you do it? How can you make work out of such horrible crimes? You're glorifying the crime." I hope I'm not – I never want to glorify. But art has to deal with all areas of humanity, all areas. Good things, bad things.

'If you think of Caravaggio or Francis Bacon or Goya – you know, we are human. I think art has to deal with all aspects of that. Mine just happens to look at the darker aspects often because I think it's a very rich area of artistic investigation.'

CHAPTER 21

THE LEGACY

THE SADDEST PART of the Easey Street saga, with all its twists, is that the two young women have almost been lost in time. Close friends who should have had lives ahead of them are now known for the brutal way in which they died rather than for who they were and what they did in life.

So, how best to remember them?

This much we know for sure: they were engaging personalities, bright women who were open and willing to learn from and share with the people around them.

Sue Bartlett's circle of friends formed through her work at the Collingwood Education Centre still see one another regularly, and they remember her well. It seems she's always in the back of their minds.

Cavell Zangalis was already teaching at the school when Sue began, through necessity on a different site. 'We were in the portables on Darling Gardens in Clifton Hill,' she recalls, sitting in her home in Hawthorn East. 'The Collingwood Girls School had been designated a high school, and in 1969 had its first intake of boys. But that school burnt down and that's when we moved to Clifton Hill.'

From her first day, the young arts and craft teacher adapted quickly to her new professional home, with its contemporary classrooms and open planning. 'She was gregarious, the kids enjoyed her sense of fun, she was alive. She didn't take life too seriously, or her work too seriously. But there was a seamless flow through her whole life; it wasn't "the teacher me" and "the friend me". She was sort of the wise woman, the ethical one,' Cavell says.

She can remember dropping round to the house in Easey Street occasionally, and meeting Suzanne Armstrong. It was a congenial place to visit. 'They were open, they enjoyed company.'

Her memory of hearing about the women's murders is more intense. Like Martin Bartlett's girlfriend at the time, she had an immediate sense of foreboding upon hearing of deaths in Easey Street. 'We were up at Mt Hotham that day in January and I put the radio on and heard the newsflash. And I just knew, I knew, it was them.' She pauses. Then, 'Oh, I still remember the shock,' she says quietly. 'So without talking much to anyone, I just said, "We're going back. We're going back." And I rushed back and it was confirmed.'

Police contacted Cavell as they tried to track down the male friend who was dating Sue. She gave them his phone number but heard nothing further.

While she claims no special knowledge of the police investigation at the time, like many who watched the inquiry unfold, she 'had a sense they sort of knew who it was but couldn't pin it and it seemed the case was sort of dropped. Certainly, all the theories we were aware of were that Sue Bartlett wasn't the target.'

'Her mother went to the grave not knowing and was tormented by it,' she says. 'She suffered terribly.'

There is one thing of which she is sure. 'Sue would have fought. She was a big girl, the adrenaline would have been flowing, she would have put up a tough fight. But it depends how she was approached; if she'd been grabbed from behind ... who knows?'

Just over a week before the women were killed, many colleagues gathered at the New Year's Eve party at 147 Easey Street. Suzie Skelton, a nurse who still lives just a couple of blocks away in Hotham Street, was there for that occasion. Like the others in attendance, she recalls a fun, low-key affair full of teachers. The evening was pleasant, she says, and people were milling around, just like most parties 'back in those days'. Good care was taken of little Greg through the evening.

Joe Blake, who taught with Sue, was also there that New Year's Eve. 'She was such a bubbly presence, the kids would've loved her, I know that,' he says. 'She was so happy and outgoing, they'd have loved it.'

He remembers the art teacher as a 'very confident' young woman. 'She was always really friendly to everyone, really outgoing.'

The moment he learnt of her death is even clearer. 'I remember seeing Susan's face on the front page of *The Age*. My wife and I were at the airport in Hobart. Horrible.'

That front page, with those overused photos, lingers in the minds of all who knew both women. Su-lin Loh has an especially powerful recollection of that edition of the newspaper. 'We were at the beach,' she says. 'Dad had gone back to work in Melbourne and he rang and told Mum; he didn't want us to just see the paper and be shocked. But I can still see their photos on the front page ... I was just shy of fifteen when it all happened, though, so mine are adolescent memories,' Su-lin is quick to emphasise.

She can also recall being at the party. A couple of weeks later, the two friends were dead. 'I remember Mum and her colleagues often wondered, "Will the police talk to us?" And they never did. There may have been nothing Mum had to say. But you'd think they would have tried to talk to as many people as possible who knew them.'

Su-lin says that, even four decades later, she and her mother often talk about Sue Bartlett, especially when they go to their beach house at Inverloch. 'It is there, it is always there, even for us who were only friends of Sue. It never goes away. So imagine what it's like for the families.

'Looking back, it's the 14-year-old me who remembers her. But if it just jogs someone else's memory or makes someone feel they can come forward [with information], it would be so good for Sue and Suzanne's families. There needs to be some justice for this terrible injustice.'

Nick Dimopoulos, who accompanied Sue Bartlett to Su-lin Loh's beach house in the 1970s, remained friends with his former partner well after they stopped dating. He still speaks with deep affection for her, even though he last saw her not long after she and Suzanne moved into Easey Street. 'It must have been in spring. I took them some flowers from my garden on my way to the Grecian Ball. Susie was a lovely girl. She loved dancing and music. She was good.'

After Sue died, he also kept in touch with her mother. 'When I got married, [she] kept coming to my shop in Ripponlea. She'd come once a week to see us. I didn't see her cry, but I tell you what – she never stopped talking about her.

'She was fantastic, she was a beautiful girl. She loved life. She did not deserve what happened. Neither of them did.'

The 77-year-old has no hesitation admitting that he cried at the funeral, or that police contacted him in 2017 to get a DNA sample. If anything, the police request reassured him they were still searching for the killer.

If Sue Bartlett was the more confident and outgoing of the pair, engaged with her teaching colleagues and the school community, Suzanne Armstrong clearly touched others in a way those who didn't even know her well still try to explain – like the neighbours who saw her with her son, waving as she dinked him on her bike, or popping over to the milk bar on the corner of Easey Street. There was something about her smile, something about the way she interacted with her son.

Half a century later, one of Suzanne's first boyfriends remembers being smitten. British-born Greg Molineaux met her when they both worked in a chemical laboratory close to Parkville, well before Suzanne's trip to Greece. They started dating, eventually moving in together in a shared house in Carlton. At the time he wanted to marry her, and he believes that, had he not returned to the United Kingdom in the late 1960s to dodge conscription in Australia, they would have done so. 'Oh, yeah. Oh, yeah, there was no doubt about it, we would have stayed together. But I didn't want to go and play the Vietnam War,' he maintains. 'I wasn't here for the allotted ballot time for my age, which I presume was twenty – I just left. The intent was for Sue to come with me, but the hiccup was that her parents wouldn't let her get a passport. So it was, "Mmm, bye, I'll be back."'

Greg Molineaux admits they didn't really keep in close contact while he was away, and by the time he returned to Melbourne, Suzanne had moved on. This still perplexes him. Nevertheless, Greg describes his former flame fondly as 'just good fun, enchanting, beautiful, friendly'.

It's not unkind to say that Suzanne's former partner is consumed by her death. He has a theory of who might have killed her, and has tried to convince police to investigate the former friend he has long suspected, but to no avail.

Colin Talbot, a respected Australian journalist, was another who believed that Suzanne had a rare charisma. He knew her as the 'swinging sixties' became the 1970s. 'Yes, we all lived in a block of flats, a three-storey block in Cromwell Street, South Yarra,' he remembered.

The writer was initially hesitant to discuss his friendship with her, not wanting to cheapen her memory by public revelation. Yet the more he recalled their time together, the more it seemed he couldn't stop talking about the smart, bright, warm woman he knew so long ago.

'Yes, she was what you might call a beautiful person,' he said, eating a late breakfast at a kerbside table outside a busy South Yarra café. 'She was a pretty girl and a beautiful person. Black hair, fit.' And young, when he knew her. 'Twenty, twenty-one, maybe.'

They had come from similar backgrounds. 'She'd come from Benalla, I'd come from the country, and we were all sort of gung-ho country kids. It takes a while to work out where you are and what you're doing. I think she ended up going round Carlton for a while, enjoying that kind of thing. I think we both started out pretty ignorant of big-city life.'

But Suzanne's engaging personality ensured she didn't remain ignorant for long. 'She was really a pretty quiet girl, but attractive. So she met people and I think as she went on and on in life, she met more and more people who probably gave her things to be interested in. So I'm not surprised she sort of soaked it all up – she was that kind of person. She was interested in all things. She had a charm about her that is relatively rare.'

Colin, at that stage a 'dogsbody journalist' at *The Australian*, managed to cadge a couple of free tickets to the opening night of the Australian Ballet's performance of *Petruska*. He believes it was at the Princess Theatre. He is more sure of Suzanne's style on this big night on the town, an 'evening dress and tux' affair if ever there was one. 'So she turned up in a gold lamé miniskirt, which was about four feet above her knees,' he said with a laugh, taken again by the vision. 'And everyone else of course was in evening dress, black tie. Initially, I was shocked. But then I thought, *Oh, that's fabulous!*'

Everyone in black tie, except, that is, for the writer. 'I was wearing a horrendous blue velvet suit that I got as a freebie. It was payola of some kind,' he said with a grin.

The pair went out a couple more times, before Talbot moved into a house in St Kilda, then up to Sydney, eventually running into Suzanne again in Carlton at 'somewhere like La Mama'.

'I was very lucky to go out with her. She was very sensitive, very nice, an extremely nice person. That's what shocked me so much – I couldn't see anybody at all deserving that, but with her it was just so unreal. She just didn't have that in her. I'm not saying she was an angel or anything ... it was the times. The pill had been invented and freed women up, and also women's lib was happening and all that other stuff, Vietnam and Christ knows what else. We were hanging around Carlton and Fitzroy and there was all the poetry at the Pram Factory. It was an exciting time.

'But the thing that struck me later, when she died, was of all the people I've ever known or gone out with, girls I've gone out with, she was as nice as anybody, anytime, anywhere. So it was particularly revolting to find out what had happened to her. I mean, I couldn't imagine it. Obviously you can't imagine that, no. It just struck me: why would someone so pure of heart really have to go through that?'

Colin Talbot passed away in October 2018 after a long illness – just months after another phone call checking in on the progress of this book. The man responsible for Suzanne and Sue's murders had to be caught: 'We've got to get him,' he would say, not joking.

What happened in Easey Street forty-two years ago will always be difficult to grasp – a cruel, preposterous violence.

Gayle Armstrong, for one, sometimes seems fractured by the loss of her older sister, almost at a loss for words about her death. Even so, she remains resolute in her determination to see the killer found. And convicted. She still lives in the same area where her family grew up, in a country cottage bursting at the seams with framed family photographs and mementos and surrounded by a lovingly tended garden. She loves to cook and concocts a delicious mulled wine, yet she doesn't stay at home for long periods, having fashioned a work schedule that ensures she's often travelling. The truth is she doesn't like being at home on her own for more than a few days at a time. Better to be out and busy.

'I'm safe here, touch wood, and it doesn't matter where I go, if I'm in trouble, if I need help, I don't have to go far to yell – or people don't have to go far to get here,' she says with a quiet laugh. 'I'm not saying "help" as in anything bad, just as in that I need somebody to get up on my roof... or if I'm not home, I can leave a key and they're all trusted to come in and do what they have to do.'

The Armstrong clan has endured great sadness. Not only did Gayle's father, Bill, die after sustaining severe injuries fighting a bushfire near Echuca, but his son – Gayle's brother Terry – died in a house fire in 2002.

But through all this turmoil, the Armstrongs kept Suzanne's son safe. He grew up in Gayle's house with her daughter and her son, who is 'the same age – two weeks' difference'.

Much was made of Greg's story on the first anniversary of the murders. Many Victorians were genuinely concerned to know how the little boy had fared, and the media was searching for a fresh angle to revisit the case. Such was the interest in his wellbeing that the state premier stepped in to promise financial compensation, after a crimes compensation tribunal initially refused the claim.

In those days, Gayle was willing to engage with reporters, to speak about Gregory or the murder of her sister. She even once spoke to a reporter as the young family visited Anglesea beach. 'As yet, we just don't know what effect the murder has had on Gregory, but at the moment he's growing up like any little boy,' she told *The Age*. 'He will grow up as my son and with his brother, Travis.' She ruminated on what Greg remembered of the night of the murders. 'It's certain he didn't see what was going on, but he must have heard something. I hope he does not remember. But we just don't know if it's out of his system.'

It certainly wasn't out of her system. Gayle made it clear she believed in an 'eye for an eye', and the broadsheet quoted her as saying that 'hanging would probably be too good for this person'. 'We'll never really get over this until this fellow is caught. You walk around not knowing who did the murder. It could be the bloke next door.'

But this kind of engagement with media has been fraught, always churning up memories and probably some hope that the talking might do some good. Shine new light on the darkest place. Her heart is still on her sleeve as she recalls those early days when Greg came to live with her family. 'I used to feed the boys in their highchairs, right here.' She gestures to the kitchen. 'They still see each other ... and Gregory goes up to see Mum a couple of times a year maybe. But they just do their own thing.'

This is a glancing reference to the fact that, at time of writing, she and Gregory are not close. She says they only see each other now 'if I happen to be there when he's seeing Mum'. She's also estranged, right now, from her younger sister, who avoids any public discussion of the case.

But Gayle is genuinely pleased that Greg is close to his father and regularly visits him in Greece. Journalist Tom Prior organised for the two to meet in Naxos, more than twenty years ago. 'That was obviously the best thing anybody could have done for Gregory, because he's become very close to that family,' his aunt reflects.

She doubts her nephew will ever want to discuss this case publicly. 'He will say to you that he probably prefers not to, because he was a baby and he doesn't remember anything, and as such it didn't affect him.' That's true, she says, 'because he keeps it back here', touching her head. 'I obviously did a very good job in bringing him up and so he got the grounding that he needed and so he's quite sensible. Very, very sensible.'

Gayle's mind tosses over myriad theories about how and why the two friends were attacked. One thing especially has always troubled her: could anyone Suzanne or the family knew really have been capable of such violence?

She is adamant that the reward offered to help solve the double murder is too paltry. 'The million dollars was not enough,' she says, defiantly. 'The million dollars was too late. It needs to be five or ten [million] now, in today's money, for somebody to come forward.'

Gayle also cannot let go of the fact that in the days and months after the murders the police didn't fully inform the Armstrong family about the investigation, or seek to build a relationship with them. 'We had to organise to go and see them. They never came to us. They never came to us. It's only all these later years – maybe, you know, one year or two years on a regular basis they have been in contact with me. Regular irregular. I think it's more of a courtesy thing now. Well, it has to be, because they haven't come back to me with anything that they may have got from that million-dollar reward.'

Almost two years after she was the 'family's face' for the launch of that reward offer, Gayle Armstrong says police had only touched base with her once. It was just after what would have been Suzanne's birthday, and while they had nothing new to report, she appreciated the gesture of keeping in contact. But she's the first to admit that she could have called them more often since the reward was posted. 'There's a lot of things I should do and I don't. And it's one of those,' she admits, with some frustration. 'I should have been on their tails ... And I should be doing more to help you ... And I realise this. I've got to be in the right state of mind. To do it.' She's reluctant to reveal too much about her job; suffice to say, it keeps her busy.

'I don't do so much because I'm waiting for the phone to ring. Is the phone going to ring? And I've got to be ready just in case the phone rings now and I've got to be gone in five minutes. That dominates. Ruled by the frigging phone.' She laughs. She also hopes that won't be the case for much longer, now that she's the proud owner of a motorhome she plans to use to get away for more relaxed stretches of time.

Meanwhile, Martin Bartlett has kept a more private vigil waiting for his older sister's murder to be solved by police. For twenty years, he had consistent, if not frequent, contact with police assigned to the case; Detective Stuart Bateson was his touchstone inside the Homicide Squad. In recent years, not so much. He expects to hear from them if and when they make headway.

But he is only too aware of how much time has passed, and so how hard it might be to find new leads, let alone a murderer who might no longer be alive. He admits that he finds it hard to talk about his sister with many others now, and he doesn't want to upset his family by referring constantly to what happened. His wife never met Susan; nor did his daughter get the chance to know her aunt.

It bothers him, too, that he can't quite remember everything that happened, that last night he was round at his sister's place. It's just out of reach, for some reason.

Just out of focus.

CHAPTER 22

THE HOPE

If the Victorian Homicide Squad can ever solve the Easey Street murders, forensic science will no doubt prove pivotal.

Back in 1977, detectives' main 'tools' were fingerprinting and blood analysis, both unreliable and at times even speculative. Now, the advances in DNA testing provide authorities with virtually irrefutable proof of identity, as long as the DNA evidence is sound.

One of Australia's prominent forensic scientists believes the progress in forensic technology makes it more possible now than ever to trace the Easey Street killer. But police need to be willing to invest in some of the new scientific processes available, financially as well as professionally. 'The key term is next-generation DNA sequencing – this is the space we need to be moving into,' he says. Whereas 'conventional DNA typing' revealed basic information, like gender, 'newer technologies can give us information on the physical make-up of a person: their eye colour, hair colour, ancestral origin and technically, any diseases they might have had'.

This kind of genetic testing has not yet been brought before the courts in Australia. But even without it, the increasing sensitivity of DNA testing generally means that it is possible to track murderers who have managed to evade police for decades. Assuming any DNA sample taken from the Easey Street crime scene has been safely stored by police, away from any moisture and sunlight, it may still be viable. Only a very small amount of DNA is needed now for testing.

Still, there could be concern about the amount of material that's left *to* test, after all this time. 'Every time I dip into a sample for testing, I have less and less of it left to use,' this expert says. 'So the decision needs to be made at some point: do we keep testing it, or hold out until more advanced methodology is available?'

While he is excited by what can still be achieved by science in this case, he has faith that the detectives working with the brief for the past twenty years have been diligent and thorough. If he was working with them now, he would suggest they cast a wide net in terms of DNA testing. This scientist is adamant that the killer is probably not one of those who were formally interviewed by the original investigating team, or the Victorian coroner.

Gladys Coventry's eyewitness account should also be given the consideration it has long deserved, he believes, pointing out that the man she reported seeing in the girls' kitchen the night they were killed was not someone she seemed to recognise. 'If her statement is true and she did see the suspect, then one of the things to take away from that is she didn't recognise him, which may or may not be anything of note – except that all of the suspects we know about have been to the house a few times at least.

'So I would almost say for sure that she didn't know this person. That's not to say that she'd necessarily know the boyfriend or anyone else that's been mentioned. It's just that all of those people would have been to the house in the recent past, so there's a chance she would have recognised them or at least hinted towards the fact that she might have seen them before.

'But she leads us more towards the fact that it's not one of these main suspects. My strong sense is that she didn't recognise the man she saw, and while none of this stands up in court, it lowers the probability of the killer being someone named in the case files.'

From a forensic perspective, the main issue is that the key suspects have been eliminated by DNA testing. 'And so my number-one suspect is the proverbial man on the grassy knoll. It's not one of these people we've been looking at for so many years.'

He also says it is unlikely that Sue and Suzanne died at the hands of a serial killer, and so examining 'copycat' crimes is a waste of time. The murderer is more likely to be a more mundane figure, perhaps a 'peeping tom' detectives overlooked back in 1977 due to the relatively insignificant nature of that offence. 'I think it's someone who has some low-level offences but has managed to avoid being put on the DNA database,' he explains. 'You've got to remember, this legislation came down in the early 2000s, so anyone who committed offences prior to that and did time, they don't retrospectively go back and get them on the database. So I'd almost be looking at a really wide dragnet of sexual offenders, as well as more petty offenders, even men who've committed break-and-enters.'

When describing 'a really wide dragnet', he is aware it is a daunting prospect; it could mean starting with a group of 10,000 people. 'I'd be looking at everyone who lived within a ten-mile radius, and if they can't do that now, then look at every known associate of the two women,' he says. 'And then everyone who lived within an arbitrary radius of their house that may have seen them regularly, seen them move in, seen them at the shops. Maybe something has struck their attention about them.'

This would entail a major workload, potentially an insurmountable one, for the current team of sixteen detectives in the cold case squad. But he argues the numbers may be culled quite quickly. 'It might be 10,000 people initially, but then you just work out who you can eliminate. That's the process I'd be going through. I'd just cut large chunks away: you know, 2000 were incarcerated, so they're gone. Look at immigration records, and perhaps another 1000 were out of the country. They're gone. And then, when I get down to whatever the lowest number is – whether it's 5000, 1000, 100 – that's where I'd start a DNA collection. A campaign of sorts, and just on a volunteer basis. That would be my approach. Given the age of the offence, you'd need to consider this approach as incorporating younger generations also, as well as employing familial DNA analysis.'

The forensic scientist also argues for a second coronial inquest into the Easey Street murders. Assuming Victorian detectives conducted a thorough cold-case review before the $1 million reward was posted in January 2017, he believes an inquest could be the only way to discover how this investigation has progressed. 'Is this investigation for all intents and purposes on ice, or is there really an active investigation going on? I don't think we've got that answer. But the only people who police have an obligation to here is Gayle Armstrong and Martin Bartlett.' If the families were to push for a new coroner's inquest, he maintains, the plea would be difficult for authorities to ignore. 'I find it baffling the first one was held so quickly. It was a double homicide: what's the point of a coronial inquest six months later? There was no need for it, and the police really had nothing to tell the coroner except that two young women had been stabbed to death. They had nothing to present in terms of information about the perpetrator. So that might be the best avenue forward: the families calling for a new coronial inquest. That will shake everything down. That's what I think is the only way to get movement.'

Looking back that far again – trying to ascertain what did and didn't happen inside 147 Easey Street on that long summer night so many, many years ago – will always be painful for Sue and Suzanne's families and friends. Was it someone they *all* knew? A man who is still in their lives? Or was it really a comparative stranger, coming through that front door on an ugly whim? Is any one scenario worse than the other?

Then there's the issue of 'closure'. If, somehow, police can arrest and charge this murderer, what then? Can justice bring peace?

For the detectives who have tried to crack this case for four decades, it seems to have been unrelentingly daunting, a tragic puzzle that defies solution.

Even those not directly involved can't let it go. As retired detective Brian Murphy thinks back to Collingwood in 1977, he's still struck by what didn't happen, what wasn't done in the original investigation. 'You've got to nurture people, look after your witnesses,' he says. 'Police are only as good as the information they've got, simple as that.'

Peter Hiscock agrees. One of the first detectives to arrive at 147 Easey Street on 13 January 1977, he will never forget the two young women who lived there, nor how they suffered as they died.

Yet he still has faith that the answer to the crime that has confounded him for four decades lies with advanced investigative techniques. 'In view of the Golden Gate investigation in the States – where they found a result with genealogy some forty-odd years later and got a serial killer and rapist off the street – I think that with saturation DNA testing we might get an answer,' he says.

The private investigator acknowledges there's 'a big possibility' that Sue and Suzanne's murderer might have died in the intervening four decades. 'It's such a long time ago and we can only theorise. But I believe it's down to investigative techniques and DNA testing of all sorts of people and possible suspects and widening the net a little bit. I think that's the only way we'll ever find him.'

Peter Hiscock is not convinced that a second coroner's inquest will achieve much in this case, and doubts it is worth pursuing. 'Does the coroner have the powers to call people to the court? I don't know whether it's going to be that strong. Honestly, I think it's down to investigative techniques.'

For the former detective who's never really left that little house in Easey Street he walked into forty-two years ago, this conviction is galvanising. And he could yet be right. At the time of writing, early in 2019, there is a sense that something could be about to happen – that police could be about to make a move in this case.

For Sue and Suzanne's sakes, let it be so.

AFTERWORD

Despite repeated requests over the past eighteen months, Victoria Police refused to discuss the Easey Street murders for this book. Nonetheless, I tried to keep them informed about my inquiries.

Had a detective from the Homicide Squad been available, these are some of the questions I would have asked:

- Was there any note made of Gladys Coventry's account of the man she alleges she saw in the women's house the night they were killed? Why wasn't an Identikit sketch made of this possible suspect? Why was there no follow-up with this witness over the next decade, while she continued to live in the house next door to the murder scene?
- Why has Peter Sellers never been formally interviewed about what he heard early on Tuesday morning, 11 January 1977?
- How thoroughly did detectives investigate Peter Collier's claim that his friend Jack Christie was the killer and had 'confessed' in group therapy at Larundel Psychiatric Hospital? Has Jack Christie's DNA been tested, either before or after his death?
- Given the police focus on John Grant as the main 'person of interest' in this matter for at least twenty years, were known

associates John Joseph Power and Anthony Collins also considered suspects? Were they DNA-tested?

- Why have key witnesses not been re-interviewed since the reward was posted?
- How many people have been DNA tested to date? Has the suspect's DNA profile been added to international databases? How long can this testing continue, given the size of the killer's DNA sample?
- Do police have a key suspect they are investigating?
- Is the cold case unit confident that they will solve the Easey Street murders?
- Realistically, how long will you continue to look into this double homicide?

NOTES

CHAPTER 1

'She even claimed she had smuggled a suitcase': Tom Prior, *They Trusted Men*. **'I am so naive sometimes'**: Tom Prior, *They Trusted Men*. **'We've just been to Athens'**: Suzanne's letter to Gayle quoted in Tom Prior, *They Trusted Men*. **'I know it will break his heart'**: Suzanne's letter to her mother and decision to leave Naxos in Tom Prior, *They Trusted Men*. **'Suzanne Armstrong had just come back from Greece'**: Comments from Sue Bartlett's brother, Martin, from author's interview with Martin Bartlett. **'The area had been split'**: Subdivision of Collingwood and 'Collingwood Flat' in Jill Barnard, 'eMelbourne: The City Past and Present' and 'Early Collingwood Memories', Collingwood Historical Society; Collingwood's population and 'noxious trades' in Jill Barnard, 'eMelbourne: The City Past and Present'. **'Charles Jardine Don ... was elected'**: 'Don, Charles Jardine (1820–1866)', Australian Trade Union Archives. **'John Wren, whose controversial career'**: 'Former John Wren's Tote', Collingwood Historical Society. **'various organisations set up to support the poor'**: Free medical dispensary and 'home for fallen women' in Jill Barnard, The Encyclopedia of Melbourne Online and 'Early Collingwood Memories', Collingwood Historical Society. **'The pervading memory that many Collingwood residents'**: Jill Barnard, The Encyclopedia of Melbourne Online. **'Ponch Hawkes, a prolific Australian photographer'**: Author's interview with Ponch Hawkes. **'By 1971, overseas-born residents'**: Jill Barnard, The Encyclopedia of Melbourne Online. **'When she and Nick came to the beach'**: Author's interview with

Su-lin Loh. **'Susan would come and babysit us'**: Author's interview with Gary Biddell. **'Every time I went over there'**: Author's interview with Martin Bartlett.

CHAPTER 2

I went over to do that': Martin Bartlett's movements that night, with girlfriend Vicki Crowe, in Martin Bartlett, police statement, 1977. **'Her brother is sure'**: Author's interview with Martin Bartlett. **'The women sustained eighty-two stab wounds'**: Police information presented to the coroner, 12 July 1977.

CHAPTER 3

'Grant was already up': Ilona's recollection of events that morning, including entering 147 Easey Street, in Ilona Stevens, police statement, 1977. ***'We have your dog which was wondering around the street'***: An image of the note is available at independentaustralia.net/australia/australia-display/exclusive-did-the-easey-street-murderer-call-tess-lawrence,9930. **'I heard the phone ring'**: Ilona's recollection of that evening in Ilona Stevens, police statement. **'I felt that there was something wrong'**: Janet Powell, police statement, 1977. **'The dog's still running around'**: Ilona's recollection of the uncollected dog and Greg's crying in author's interview with Ilona Stevens.

CHAPTER 4

'Because there were two of them': Author's interview with Peter Hiscock. **'On the bedspread near the window'**: Description of crime scene, theories on killer and quotations from Detective Senior Sergeant Alf Oldfield, statement to the coroner. **'I clearly remember the bed'**: Description of crime scene, theories on killer and quotations taken from author's interview with Peter Hiscock.

CHAPTER 5

'The sink was dry, the stove was turned off': Description of crime scene and quotations taken from Henry Huggins, statement to the coroner. **'The final list of exhibits'**: Taken from Huggins, statement to the coroner and Moira McBain, statement to the coroner. **'A Constable Ron Iddles had stopped a man in a car'**: Justine Ford, *The Good Cop*. **'spermatozoa were found on both swabs'**: Evidence presented to the coroner taken from Huggins, statement to the coroner. **'would not "make the grade"'**: Author's interview with Henry Huggins. **'167 centimetres in height and weighing 60 kilograms'**: James McNamara, statement to the coroner.

CHAPTER 6

'Suzanne Armstrong's mother Eileen found out': 'Today', Channel Nine. **'Sue Bartlett's brother Martin'**: Author's interview with Martin Bartlett. **'Gayle Armstrong was 1000 kilometres away'**: News of sister's death and visit to the Woodard brothers from author's interview with Gayle Armstrong. **'contains no graves'**: 'Tilpa', Australian Cemeteries Index. **'Gayle's a wild one'**: Barry Woodard quoted in Tom Prior, *They Trusted Men*. **'It was terrible'**: Author's interview with Gayle Armstrong. **'I had to'**: Author's interview with Martin Bartlett. **'I would like there to be no minimising of the brutality'**: Quoted in Mike Roberts, 'Public Fill a Chapel for Victims' Funeral'. **'Obviously, at that stage there was an ongoing inquiry'**: Author's interview with Martin Bartlett.

CHAPTER 7

'She had been with me at my sister's place': Quotations from Barry Woodard in this chapter taken from Barry Woodard, police statement, 1977. **'Barry has been with me for a few years'**: Quotations from Margaret Chilcott in this chapter taken from Margaret Chilcott, police statement, 1977. **'But I could not understand it'**: Henry Woodard, police statement, 1977. **'An American friend of mine walked into my room'**: Visit and quotations in Tom Prior, *They Trusted Men*.

CHAPTER 8

'They were very innocent times': Helen Garner, 'Cold Case Confidential'. **'It used to be wide open'**: Philip's recollection of playing with Greg and of Collingwood from author's interview with Phillip Perez. **'He didn't understand'**: Author's interview with Josephine Perez. **'It was either a dream or someone walking past'**: Author's interview with Christina Fourtouris.

CHAPTER 9

'They buggered it up': Murphy's view of Gladys Coventry and the investigation from author's interview with Brian Murphy. **'charged (and acquitted) of homicide'**: John Silvester, 'As a Detective, Brian Murphy Refused to Follow the Book. Now He's Writing His Own'. **'Dr Birrell, renowned around the world'**: Andrew Rule, 'Police Surgeon John Birrell Saved Lives with His Battle to Get Laws to Make Our Roads Safer'. **'I think he told her he'd come for a welfare check'**: Murphy's view of John Birrell from author's interview with Brian Murphy. **'a really poor quality lean-to'**: Hugh's memories of Gladys, her house and her revelations about the murders from author's interview with Hugh Parry-Jones. **'couldn't complain about living in Easey Street'**: Author's interview with Edie Haines. **'I was on holidays too'**: Peter's recollections of the evening of the murders, police follow-up and call to Crime Stoppers from author's interview with Peter Sellers. **'I pushed Peter to call'**: Author's interview with Robyn McKenzie. **'That's rubbish'**: Author's interview with Bob Sellers.

CHAPTER 10

'Police launched a man-hunt in Collingwood', **'She was naked from the waist down'**, **'looking for a crazed sex killer'**: Ron Connelly, '2 Women Knifed to Death'. **'murder house'**: Tony Wilson, 'Baby Alone in Murder House'. **'The boyfriend of one of two young women'**: Gerry Carman and Michael Gordon, 'Bodies Two Days in Death House'. **'Roving shearer Barry Woodard'**: Gerry Carman and Michael Gordon, 'Violent Death Ended a Christmas Love Story'. **'[stabbed] at least 40 times'**: Ron Connelly, '2 Women Knifed to Death'. **'a very, very sick person'**: Inspector Noel Jubb quoted in Rowan Forster, 'It Remains One of Our Most Baffling Unsolved Cases. Who Killed Easey Street Residents Susan Bartlett and Suzanne Armstrong?' **'They do not want their information released'**: Gerry Carman, 'Double Killing: Two Leads'. **'The knife was … discovered'**: Michael Gordon, 'Knife Murder Clue'. **'There are no blood samples on the knife'**: Michael Gordon, 'Knife Murder Clue'. **'the killer spent some time inside the house'**: 'Easey St Murders Appeal'. **'With a sex killer like this at large'**: Chief Inspector Don Plant quoted in Tony Wilson, 'Baby Alone in Murder House'. **'I know two wrongs don't make a right'**, **'If only people would realise'**: Bill Armstrong and Martin Bartlett quoted in Tess Lawrence, 'A Broker, A Father Amid Broken Dreams'. **'I was grilled at one stage'**: Quotations from Barry Woodard in Richard Shears, 'I Want to Look After My Dead Girl's Boy, Says Barry'. **'The horror of that morning'**: Owen McKenna, 'My Day of Horror – Exclusive – Girl Next Door Tells'. **'The trousers were dry-cleaned'**: Jack Ayling, 'Blood Soaked Trousers Clue'. **'Detective Senior Sergeant Alf Oldfield told *Truth*'**: Ian Dougall, title unknown, *Truth*. **'Now all Gayle feels is an emptiness'**: Richard Shears, 'Suzanne's Gregory is Doing Just Fine'.

CHAPTER 11

'Crime rounds were different then': Author's interview with undisclosed source. **'in the wrong spot twice'**: Author's interview with Peter Hiscock. **'the result of homicide'**: Sara Hinchey quoted in Tammy Mills, '"It was murder"'. **'the real *bad* deal'**: Author's interview with undisclosed source. **'Collins and Grant came over'**: Tammy Mills, '"It was murder"'. **'a view to having him wrongfully charged'**: Powers' allegations and their substantiation by Barry Beach QC in Beach, 'Report of the Board of Inquiry into Allegations against Members of the Victoria Police Force'. **'Power was dying'**: Nino Bucci, 'Another Twist in the Julie Ann Garciacelay Cold Case, 40 Years After She Disappeared'. **'We went over there for a drink'**: John Grant quoted in ibid. **'They came all the way to see me'**: Author's interview with Adrian Tame. **'It is understood, too'**: Author's undisclosed source. **'We didn't have that kind of relationship'**: Ilona's recollections of John Grant and the night of the murders from author's interview with Ilona Stevens. **'They never came the house'**: Author's interview with undisclosed source. **'matters of life and death'**: Geoffrey Barker, 'The Crumbling Estate'. **'a very brutal murder'**: Harry Pascoe quoted in title unknown, *The Herald*.

CHAPTER 12

'special session': Gayle Armstrong's impressions of her encounter with Doris Stokes from author's interview with Gayle Armstrong. **'I woke up and saw'**: Doris Stokes' session with Gayle Armstrong and quotations from Stokes in Stephen O'Baugh, 'Psychic "Speaks" to Murder Victim'. **'concerned with the natural'**: Chief Inspector Paul Delianis quoted in 'Murder Séance Not On: Police'. **'I had contact with Lorraine's father'**: Quoted in Tom Prior, *They Trusted Men*. **'Yeah, those girls went into the house'**: Author's interview with Gayle Armstrong. **'They got police off-side'**: Author's interview with Debbie Malone. **'worked "with the assistance of police"'**: 'Presenter – Debbie Malone', *Oz Paranormal and Spiritual Expo*, 2018, www.ozparaexpo.com.au/ldquobetween-two-worldsrdquo-with-debbie-malone.html. **'The community has a broader appreciation'**: Author's interview with Debbie Malone. **'She told me I was going to travel'**: Author's interview with Gayle Armstrong.

CHAPTER 13

'Like some of the police involved': Prior's motivation to write about the case, representation of the two women, recounting of Suzanne's time in Greece, interview with Greg Armstrong and theories about the killer taken from Tom Prior, *They Trusted Men*. **'Owen was a drinker, a gambler'**: Tom Prior, *They Trusted Men*. **'Towards the end, Tom met that cop'**: Author's interview with Michael Wilkinson. **'What Prior didn't write'**: Andrew Rule, 'No Easey Answers Forty Years After Women Slain'.

CHAPTER 14

'the monster was genuinely shocked': Tom Prior, *They Trusted Men*. **'Dear Bruce'**: quotations from Peter Collier's letters, dated 30 January 2004, 11 February 2004, 23 January 2004, n.d. March 2004 and n.d. July 2004. **'The**

initial intake of 387 patients expanded': History of Larundel, 'Larundel Mental Asylum', Darebin Heritage. **'Your [sic] probably aware'**: Peter Collier, 10 January 2007. **'out of the blue'**: Author's interview with Gayle Armstrong. **'We support each other'**: Bruce Kimball quoted in Sue Hewitt, 'Mum's Cold Case Quest'. **'lived in just a bark or a tin hut'**: Author's interview with undisclosed source. **'You can be sued'**: Author's interview with Lester Walton.

CHAPTER 15

'I think for a story not to be resolved': Helen Garner, 'Cold Case Confidential'. **'a shabby holiday town'**: Andrew Rule, *Rule on Crime*. **'I remember being called'**: Ron Iddles quoted in Justine Ford, *The Good Cop*. **'I think it is important'**: Iddles quoted in Keith Moor, 'Victoria Police Cold Case Unit Identifies 30 Homicide Cases They Believe Are "Highly Solvable"'. **'getting great results'**: Iddles quoted in Keith Moor, 'Cold Case Murders'. **'too many "persons of interest"'**: Author's interview with Iddles. **'the DNA testing hadn't been done correctly', 'While DNA testing has so far failed to uncover an offender'**: Bruce Currie and Iddles quoted in Chris Vedelago, 'New DNA Testing for Easey Street Suspects'. **'a long, long story'**: Iddles quoted in AAP, 'New Lead in 1977 Vic Easey St Murders'.

CHAPTER 16

'the most beautiful X-ray photographs': History of DNA in 'The History of DNA Timeline', *DNA WorldWide*. **'Jeffreys quickly realised'**: Jeffreys' discovery and the Colin Pitchfork and Desmond Applebee cases in Ian Cobain, 'Killer Breakthrough – The Day DNA Evidence First Nailed a Murderer'. **'a Melbourne serial rapist, George Kaufman'**: Keith Moor, 'Cold Case Murders'. **'24 hours, seven days a week'**: 'National Criminal Investigation DNA Database', Australian Criminal Intelligence Commission. **'1936 samples from the scenes'**: Keith Moor, 'Cold Case Sex Attacks'. **'68,000 attempts to match profiles'**: Quotations and reporting of proposal to store genetic samples in Paul Gregoire and Ugur Nedim, 'The National DNA Database is Watching You'. **'Golden State Killer'**: Benjamin Oreskes et al., 'False Starts in Search for Golden State Killer Reveal the Pitfalls of DNA

Testing'. **'four bodies found in two barrels'**: New Hampshire Public Radio, Bearbookpodcast.com. **'did not "currently use online genealogy databases"'**: Erin Pearson, 'Beware! Cops Can Use DNA Data to Pick Bad Apples from Your Family Tree'.

CHAPTER 17

'been before the coroner': '8 Victorian Cold Case Deaths Draw $1 Million Rewards for Information'. **'sadness of not knowing where she is'**: AAP, 'Victoria Police Offers $8 Million in Rewards to Solve Cold Cases'. **'the rewards system was being overhauled'**: Robert Baird, 'Victoria Police Overhauls Rewards System for Serious Crime'. **'comfort and hope'**: Role of rewards and statistics on payouts in Ugur Nedim, 'Catching Criminals'. **'In the past thirty or forty years'**: Author's interview with Ron Iddles. **'help solve crimes', 'paid for providing evidence'**: Nick Howe and Tim Passmore quoted in Emma Hallett, 'Do Cash Rewards Actually Help Catch Criminals?' **'The media has a big part to play'**: Iddles quoted in Keith Moor, 'Cold Case Murders'. **'here's a million dollars', 'the mistakes those guys may have made'**: Gayle Armstrong and Mick Hughes quoted in Luke Costin, '$1m Reward for 1977 Easey Street Murders'. **'If you're going to offer your DNA'**: Hughes quoted in Loretta Florance, 'Easey Street Murders'. **'Everything, everything'**: Armstrong quoted in Luke Costin, '$1m Reward for 1977 Easey Street Murders'. **'We have good DNA evidence'**: Hughes quoted in 'Million-dollar Reward Offered for Information on Easey St Murders'. **'all concerning people like me'**: Armstrong quoted in Loretta Florance, 'Easey Street Murders'.

CHAPTER 18

'come forward now': Jenny Rose Ng murder recounted in AAP, 'Fresh Appeal to Solve 30-year Murder', *News.com.au*. **'Andrew Rule reported'**: Neil Rowland Bugg's story in Andrew Rule, 'No Easey Answers Forty Years After Women Slain'. **'I could smell their blood in the hallway'**: Tess Lawrence, 'Did the Easey Street Murderer Call Tess Lawrence?'

CHAPTER 19

'It's very different to homicide involving intimate partners': Author's interview with Professor Debbie Kirkwood. **'"organised/disorganized" serial killers'**: Robert Ressler et al., 'Sexual Killers and Their Victims', pp. 288–308. **'an examination of the crime scene'**: David Canter et al., 'The Organized/ Disorganized Typology of Serial Murder'. **'revised classification model'**: Richard D. Keppel and Richard Walter, 'Profiling Killers', pp. 417–37.

CHAPTER 20

'Peter Demeris had bought the house': See realestateview.com.au. **'It was difficult to sell'**: Chris Vedelago, 'Notorious Murder House Changes Hands'. **'the owner's got tradies in'**: Author's interview with Hugh Parry-Jones. **'I suppose it would have helped to actually know up front'**: Dennis Gentry quoted in Natalie Harris, '147 Easey Street'. **'This strange note'**: Author's interview with Dean Wilson. **'Larundel Hospital protected Anthony Thomas Christie'**: Note by Peter Collier, given to the author by Andrew Muir. **'the street was still abuzz'**: Author's interview with Susy Potter. **'More than 100 people turned up for the sale'**: Bruce Kimball and Bill Batcheler quoted in Chris Vedelago, 'Notorious Murder House Changes Hands'. **'Enjoying a revitalised identity'**: Nelson Alexander, '147 Easey Street', realestate.com.au. **'They were always up there'**: Recollections of the murder and the neighbourhood, and theories on the killer, from author's interview with Andrew Muir. **'I moved into this student house'**: Recollections of the neighbourhood from author's interview with Steve Cox.

CHAPTER 21

'We were in the portables on Darling Gardens': Recollections of Sue Bartlett from author's interview with Cavell Zangalis. **'The evening was pleasant, she says'**: Recollections of party from author's interview with Susie Skelton. **'She was such a bubbly presence'**: Recollections of Sue Bartlett from author's interview with Joe Blake. **'We were at the beach'**: Recollections of Sue Bartlett and news of death from author's interview with Su-lin Loh. **'It must have been in spring'**: Recollections of Sue Bartlett and news of death from author's interview with Nick Dimopoulos. **'we would have stayed together'**: Recollections of Suzanne Armstrong from author's interview with Greg Molineaux. **'we all lived in a block of flats'**: Recollections of Suzanne Armstrong and bohemian Melbourne from author's interview with Colin Talbot. **'I'm safe here, touch wood'**: Author's interview with Gayle Armstrong. **'Terry's death also made headlines'**: 'Trail of Sadness'. **'Martin Bartlett has kept a more private vigil'**: Author's interview with Martin Bartlett.

CHAPTER 22

'The key term is next-generation DNA sequencing': Forensic scientist's comments on DNA testing and the Easey Street case from author's interview with undisclosed source. **'You've got to nurture people'**: Author's interview with Brian Murphy. **'with saturation DNA testing we might get an answer'**: Author's interview with Peter Hiscock.

BIBLIOGRAPHY

BOOKS AND ARTICLES

'8 Victorian Cold Case Deaths Draw $1 Million Rewards for Information', *ABC News*, 6 June 2015.

'Don, Charles Jardine (1820–1866)', Australian Trade Union Archives, 5 February 2002, www.atua.org.au/biogs/ALE1116b

'Early Collingwood Memories', Collingwood Historical Society, n.d., collingwoodhs.org.au/wp-content/uploads/3-Early-Collingwood-Memories-In-Those-Days.pdf

'Easey St Murders Appeal', *The Melbourne Times*, 19 January 1977.

'Easey Street Murders: Million-dollar Reward Offered for Information on Easey St Murders', *Herald Sun*, 14 January 2017.

'Former John Wren's Tote', Collingwood Historical Society, n.d., www.collingwoodhs.org.au/resources/collingwood-history-plaques-project/former-john-wrens-tote/

'Larundel Mental Asylum', Darebin Heritage, www.heritage.darebinlibraries.vic.gov.au/article/328

'Murder Séance Not On: Police', *The Sun*, 26 June 1978.

'National Criminal Investigation DNA Database', Australian Criminal Intelligence Commission, 2 November 2018, www.acic.gov.au/our-services/biometric-and-forensic-services/national-criminal-investigation-dna-database

'The History of DNA Timeline', *DNA WorldWide*, 13 August 2016.

'Tilpa', Australian Cemeteries Index, 7 June 2017, http://austcemindex.com/cemetery?cemid=2164.

'Trail of Sadness', *The Border Mail*, 21 September 2002.

AAP, 'Fresh Appeal to Solve 30-year Murder', *News.com.au*, 23 April 2012.

——, 'New Lead in 1977 Vic Easey St Murders', *News.com.au*, 26 February 2014.

——, 'Victoria Police Offers $8 Million in Rewards to Solve Cold Cases', *The Age*, 6 June 2015.

Ayling, Jack, 'Blood Soaked Trousers Clue', *Truth*, 22 January 1977.

Baird, Robert, 'Victoria Police Overhauls Rewards System for Serious Crime', *ABC Online*, 25 March 2015.

Barker, Geoffrey, 'The Crumbling Estate', *Griffith Review*, vol. 25, Spring 2009, pp. 44–48.

Barnard, Jill, 'eMelbourne: The City Past and Present', *The Encyclopedia of Melbourne Online*, 2018, www.emelbourne.net.au/biogs/EM00375b.htm.

Bucci, Nino, 'Another Twist in the Julie Ann Garciacelay Cold Case, 40 Years After She Disappeared', *The Age*, 1 July 2015.

Canter, David et al., 'The Organized/Disorganized Typology of Serial Murder: Myth or Model?', *Psychology, Public Policy and Law*, vol. 10, no. 3, September 2004, pp. 293–320.

Carman, Gerry and Gordon, Michael, 'Bodies Two Days in Death House', *The Age*, 14 January 1977, p. 1.

——, 'Violent Death Ended a Christmas Love Story', *The Age*, 14 January 1977.

Carman, Gerry, 'Double Killing: Two Leads', *The Age*, 15 January 1977.

Cobain, Ian, 'Killer Breakthrough – The Day DNA Evidence First Nailed a Murderer', *The Guardian*, 8 June 2016.

Connelly, Ron, '2 Women Knifed to Death', *The Herald*, 13 January 1977, p. 1.

Costin, Luke, '$1m Reward for 1977 Easey Street Murders', *SBS News*, 15 January 2017.

Florance, Loretta, 'Easey Street Murders: $1m Reward to Catch Cold Case Killer Who Left Toddler Alone in Cot', *ABC News*, 16 January 2017.

Ford, Justine, *The Good Cop: The True Story of Ron Iddles, Australia's Greatest Detective*, Pan Macmillan, Sydney, 2016.

Forster, Rowan, 'It Remains One of Our Most Baffling Unsolved Cases. Who Killed Easey Street Residents Susan Bartlett and Suzanne Armstrong?', *Herald Sun*, 28 July 2015.

Gordon, Michael, 'Knife Murder Clue', *The Age*, 21 January 1977.

Gregoire, Paul and Nedim, Ugur, 'The National DNA Database is Watching You', *Sydney Criminal Lawyers*, 24 February 2017.

Hallett, Emma, 'Do Cash Rewards Actually Help Catch Criminals?', *BBC News*, 24 June 2014.

Hewitt, Sue, 'Mum's Cold Case Quest', *Herald Sun*, 20 September 2009.

Keppel, Richard D. and Walter, Richard, 'Profiling Killers: A Revised Classification Model for Understanding Sexual Murder', *International Journal of Offender Therapy and Comparative Criminology*, vol. 43, no. 4, 1 December 1999, pp. 417–37.

Lawrence, Tess, 'A Broker, A Father Amid Broken Dreams', *The Herald*, 21 January 1977.

——, 'Did the Easey Street Murderer Call Tess Lawrence?', *Independent Australia*, 17 January 2017.

McKenna, Owen, 'My Day of Horror – Exclusive – Girl Next Door Tells', *Truth*, 22 January 1977.

Mills, Tammy, '"It Was Murder": 1975 Missing Librarian Case Revolves Around Boxer, Violent Criminal and Crime Reporter', *The Age*, 12 April 2018.

Moor, Keith, 'Cold Case Murders: The Crimes That Keep Top Homicide Detective Ron Iddles Awake at Night', *Herald Sun*, 17 February 2017.

——, 'Cold Case Sex Attacks: DNA Profiles Matched to More Than 80 Rapists in Victoria', *Herald Sun*, 3 March 2017.

——, 'Victoria Police Cold Case Unit Identifies 30 Homicide Cases They Believe Are "Highly Solvable"', *Herald Sun*, 19 March 2013.

Nedim, Ugur, 'Catching Criminals: Do Rewards Really Work?', *Sydney Criminal Lawyers*, 30 March 2015.

O'Baugh, Stephen, 'Psychic "Speaks" to Murder Victim', *The Sunday Press*, 25 June 1978.

Oreskes, Benjamin; Serna, Joseph and Winton, Richard, 'False Starts in

Search for Golden State Killer Reveal the Pitfalls of DNA Testing', *Los Angeles Times*, 4 May 2018.

Pearson, Erin, 'Beware! Cops Can Use DNA Data to Pick Bad Apples from Your Family Tree', *The Sydney Morning Herald*, 5 July 2018.

Prior, Tom, *They Trusted Men: The Untold Story of the Easey Street Murders*, Wilkinson Books, Melbourne, 1996.

Ressler, Robert et al., 'Sexual Killers and Their Victims: Identifying Patterns Through Crime Scene Analysis', *Journal of Interpersonal Violence*, vol.1, no. 3, 1 September 1986, pp. 288–308.

Roberts, Mike, 'Public Fill a Chapel for Victims' Funeral', *The Age*, 21 January 1977.

Rule, Andrew, 'No Easey Answers Forty Years After Women Slain', *Herald Sun*, 2 June 2018.

——, 'Police Surgeon John Birrell Saved Lives with His Battle to Get Laws to Make Our Roads Safer', *Herald Sun*, 19 June 2016.

——, *Rule on Crime: 10 Crime Stories You Won't Forget*, Wilkinson Publishing, 2017.

Shears, Richard, 'I Want to Look After My Dead Girl's Boy, Says Barry', *The Sunday Press*, 16 January 1977.

——, 'Suzanne's Gregory is Doing Just Fine', *The Sunday Press*, 15 May 1977.

Silvester, John, 'As a Detective, Brian Murphy Refused to Follow the Book. Now He's Writing his Own', *The Age*, 7 September 2017, www.smh.com.au/opinion/as-a-detective-brian-murphy-refused-to-follow-the-book-now-hes-writing-his-own-20170907-gycpym.html

Vedelago, Chris, 'New DNA Testing for Easey Street Suspects', *The Age*, 8 April 2013.

——, 'Notorious Murder House Changes Hands', *The Age*, 21 August 2011.

Wilson, Tony, 'Baby Alone in Murder House', *The Sun*, 14 January 1977.

INTERVIEWS

Armstrong, Gayle, multiple interviews, June 2017 to December 2018.
Bartlett, Martin, multiple interviews, December 2017 to December 2018.
Biddle, Gary, August 2018.
Blake, Joe, March 2018.
Cox, Steve, November 2017.
Dimopoulos, Nick, April 2018.
Fourtouris, Christina, December 2017.
Haines, Edie, August 2018.
Hawkes, Ponch, July 2018.
Hiscock, Peter, July 2017 to December 2018.
Huggins, Henry, May 2018.
Iddles, Ron, multiple interviews, July to November 2017.
Kirkwood, Debbie, August 2018.
Lawrence, Tess, January 2019.
Loh, Su-lin, April 2018.
Malone, Debbie, March 2018.
McKenzie, Robyn, March 2018.
Molineaux, Greg, July 2017.
Muir, Andrew, December 2017.
Murphy, Brian, multiple interviews, February to September 2018.
Parry-Jones, Hugh, March 2018.
Perez, Josephine, November 2017.
Perez, Phillip, November 2017.
Potter, Susy, August 2018.
Sellers, Bob, March 2018.
Sellers, Peter, March 2018.
Skelton, Susie, March 2018.
Stevens, Ilona, multiple interviews, May 2017 to September 2018.
Talbot, Colin, January 2018.
Tame, Adrian, multiple interviews, December 2017 to April 2018.
Walton, Lester, June 2018.
Wilkinson, Michael, November 2017.

Wilson, Dean, August 2018.
Woodard, Barry, request for interview, November 2017.
Zangalis, Cavell, March 2018.

REPORTS, LETTERS AND POLICE FILES

Beach, Barry Watson, 'Report of the Board of Inquiry into Allegations against Members of the Victoria Police Force', volume 1, May 1978.
Letters from Peter Collier, dated 30 January 2004, 11 February 2004, 23 February 2004, n.d. March 2004, n.d. July 2004 and 10 January 2007, reproduced with kind permission of Gayle Armstrong.
Original note from Barry Woodard, January 1977, in police files.
Statements in the police brief to the coroner from Barry Woodard, Henry Woodard, Ilona Stevens, Janet Powell, Margaret Chilcott and Martin Bartlett, all dated 12 July 1977, Public Records Office Victoria.
Statements to the coroner from Alf Oldfield, James McNamara, Henry Huggins and Moira McBain, 12 July 1977, Public Records Office Victoria.

TELEVISION AND RADIO PROGRAMS

Thomas, Helen, 'Cold Case Confidential', *Background Briefing*, ABC Radio National, 15 May 2005.
Harris, Natalie, '147 Easey Street', *Vice Cool City*, Vimeo, 8 June 2011.
New Hampshire Public Radio, 2018 Bearbookpodcast.com

ACKNOWLEDGEMENTS

This book could not have been written without the insight of many of the people deeply affected by the deaths of Susan Bartlett and Suzanne Armstrong.

I am most indebted to Gayle Armstrong and Martin Bartlett for their time and patience over the past eighteen months, as we looked back again at what happened on the night of 10 January 1977. These discussions were never easy, yet they persevered – always with dignity, and sometimes even gentle humour.

Special thanks to Ilona Stevens, too, for her unstinting resolve to remember all she could about her old neighbours, and Peter Hiscock, who always found a way to fit one more chat in to his allegedly 'semi-retired' private investigator's schedule. The unique perspectives of Ron Iddles, Brian Murphy and Adrian Tame also proved invaluable.

My thanks to the neighbours, past and present, who helped bring Easey Street into fresh focus; to Sue's and Suzanne's friends, who were so willing to share their memories; and to Gina Cidoni.

More personally, I'm grateful to Peter Bridges and Kay Dyson for their hospitality when I stayed in Melbourne doing this research;

'first reader' Marian Frith; and, as always, lioness Lyn Tranter. My journalistic colleague Andrew Rule deserves mention too, for his astute 'riding instructions' throughout this assignment.

The team at Black Inc. have also been supportive throughout this investigation, especially editor Julia Carlomagno, publisher Caitlin Yates and former associate publisher Julian Welch, who believed so strongly that Sue and Suzanne's murders had to be examined again.

Printed in the USA
CPSIA information can be obtained
at www.ICGtesting.com
LVHW041118240924
791856LV00002B/385